The Dutch in Bengal and Bihar
1740-1825 A.D.

THE DUTCH IN BENGAL AND BIHAR

1740-1825 A.D.

DR. KALIKINKAR DATTA

MOTILAL BANARSIDASS PUBLISHERS
PRIVATE LIMITED • DELHI

Reprint : Delhi, 2017
Second Revised & Enlarged Edition, 1968

ISBN : 978-81-208-4039-3

Motilal Banarsidass
41 U.A., Bungalow Road, Jawahar Nagar, Delhi 110 007
8 Mahalaxmi Chamber, 22 Bhulabhai Desai Road, Mumbai 400 026
203 Royapettah High Road, Mylapore, Chennai 600 004
236, 9th Main III Block, Jayanagar, Bengaluru 560 011
8 Camac Street, Kolkata 700 017
Ashok Rajpath, Patna 800 004
Chowk, Varanasi 221 001

MLBD Cataloging-in-Publication Data
The Dutch in Bengal and Bihar
by DR. KALIKINKAR DATTA
ISBN : 978-81-208-4039-3
Includes Appendices, Bibliography,
Glossary and Index
I. History II. Politics III. Relations Between
Dutch and English in Bengal and Bihar
V. Datta, Kalikinkar

Printed in India
by RP Jain at NAB Printing Unit,
A-44, Naraina Industrial Area, Phase I, New Delhi–110028
and published by JP Jain for Motilal Banarsidass Publishers (P) Ltd,
41 U.A. Bungalow Road, Jawahar Nagar, Delhi-110007

TABLE OF CONTENTS

PREFACE

The middle of the eighteenth century was marked by a tragic turn in the political destiny of India. The tragedy was caused by a number of disintegrating influences which followed as a logical sequel to the decline of central political authority and lack of sound governance. Internal disorders and insolvency of this country not only excited the greed of Asiatic invaders like Nadir Shah and Ahmad Shah. Abdali, but also emboldened the European trading companies like the English, the French and the Dutch to convert this land into one of the theatres of their hostilities, which were, to a large extent, echoes of their rivalries in other parts of the world. It is well known how of the three competiting nations the English at last emerged completely successful with seeds of their supremacy carefully sown by them on the fertile soils of Bengal and the Carnatic. British capture of Chandernagore, the most important French settlement in Bengal, in March, 1757, and their victory at Vandivas in January, 1760, were certainly very significant events facilitating the rise of British political authority in this country. The battle of Bedara also greatly supplemented this process and so there is perfect justification in describing it as one of the decisive battles of Indian History. Dutch influence in Bengal was henceforth crippled beyond any chance of recovery, and under the pressure of some Indian and extra-Indian forces, it completely vanished by the year 1825.

We read the story of the expulsion of the French from Bengal in Malleson's **'History of the French in India'**, *S. C. Hill's* **'Three Frenchmen in Bengal'**. *Edward Ives'* **'Voyage'**, **'Memoir of M. Jean Law'**, *Orme's* **'History of the Military Transactions of the British Nation in Indostan'**, **'Siyar-ul-mutakherin'** *and some other published as well as unpublished works. But the history of the decline of Dutch influence in Bengal and other parts of India was not adequately known to us. I feel I have not been able to present, because of various adverse circumstances, such a complete picture as would have been possible after a comprehensive utilization of all relevant materials from different collections in and outside India. But I have tried my best to prepare my account by carefully pieceing together bits of information culled from a variety of sources available in our country. I crave indulgence of my learned readers for the imperfections of this work of which no one is more conscious than myself.*

I am thankful to Shri K. C. Banerjee M. A., and to Shri Tara Saran Sinha, M. A., for their kindness in going through the proofs and preparing the Index respectively.

The Dutch in Bengal and Bihar, 1740-1825 A. D.

CHAPTER I

Early Relationships

Dutch Settlements, and the Council at Chinsura

Like the English and the French, the Dutch had considerable commercial transactions in India[1]. At different dates since their advent here, they managed to secure *farmans*, *parwanahs*[2] and agreements, in favour of their trade, from the Mughal imperial government, its provincial Viceroys and many local chiefs, in almost all parts of the country[3]. They established factories within the jurisdiction of the Bengal *subah* not only at important centres of commerce, such as Pipli, Balasore, Patna, Futwah, Dacca, Maldah, Kalikapur near Cassimbazar, Chinsura and Baranagore, and Jugdea or Luckipur, but also at some villages in the interior[4] with the object of collecting in sufficient quantities the various species of goods, required for their

---

1. Milburn, Oriental Commerce, Vol. II, pp. 338-380.

2. Vide my paper on 'A Parwanah of Shuja-ud-din Muhammad Khan to the Dutch' published in Proceedings of the Indian Historical Records Commission, 21st Session.

3. Several years back I obtained from the I. R. D., now known as National Archives of India, New Delhi, transcripts of some documents (translated from Dutch into English) containing terms of treaties concluded by the Dutch with Indian rulers and chiefs, and of the farmans, etc., granted by the latter to them between 1612 and 1773.

4. "They (the Marathas) plundered the factories of the Dutch at Kagaram and Mowgrama". Maharastrpurana. In 1789 the Dutch established a sugar facory at Motipur (about 18 miles north of Muzaffarpur in north Bihar).

investments, from the original places of production[1].

In 1627 the Dutch Governor of Coromandel deputed some men to Bengal to establish a trading station there. For sometime it remained subordinate to the Coromandel establishment, but in view of its increasing importance the Government of Batavia created in 1655 a separate organisation known as the Directorate of Bengal. Already in 1653 the Dutch had established a settlement at Chinsura. Bernier (1665-66) mentions Dutch establishments in *Bengale* (Bengal), or at Patna [2]. Referring to Bengal as the "common storehouse" for cotton and silk "not of *Hindoustan* (Hindustan) or the Empire of the Great *Moghul* only, but of all the neighbouring kingdoms and even of Europe", he observes : "I have been sometimes amazed at the vast quantity of cotton cloths, of every sort, fine and coarse, white and coloured which the *Hollånders* alone export to different places, especially to Japan and Europe....The Dutch have sometimes seven or eight hundred natives employed in their silk factory at *Kassem-Bazar* (Cassimbazar), where, in like manner, the English and other merchants employ a proportionate number" [3]. The Dutch also exported "a prodigious quantity" of saltpetre from Patna[4]. Tavernier, who stayed at Patna for eight days (21st to 28th December, 1665), writes: "The Dutch Company has an establishment there on account of the trade in saltpetre which it refines at a large village called

1. In the economic order prevailing in Bengal in those days the industrial activities of her people, especially in relation to cotton manufacture, were widespread and extensive. In fact, the weaving manufactories "were dispersed throughout the country", and not only the big cities but also many villages in distant corners were flourishing centres of cotton manufacture. This accounts for the establishment of factories and aurungs at such places by the European trading Companies. There was a tremendous growth in the number of English factories during the post-Plassey period. Mir Qasim observed in one of his letters addressed to the English Governor in Calcutta in May 1762; "Near four or five hundred new factories have been established in my dominions and it is impossible to express what disturbances are made in every factory and how the inhabitants are oppressed". Vansittart's Narrative. Vol. II., pp. 97-102.

2. Francois Bernier, Travels in the Mogul Empire, edited by Constable, p. 293.

3. Ibid, pp. 439-440.

4. Ibid.

Chapra, situated on the right bank of the Ganges, 10 *coss* above Patna" [1]. He also saw a *very fine house* built by the Dutch at Dacca for safe storage of their goods. John Marshall (1662-72 A. D.) describes the Dutch factory at Pipli [2] as '*handsome*' and that at Hugli as 'stately' [3]. He also notes that the Dutch Factory at Cassimbazar, located at a distance of about one mile from the English factory there, was '*very large*' with '*handsome gardens belonging to it*' [4]. Strenshyam Master was entertained in the Dutch factory at Cassimbazar on the 30th September, 1676 and he was highly impressed with its buildings and gardens [5]. By 1676 the Dutch had deserted their factory at Pipli and built a new one at Balasore. Under the Directorate of Bengal there were then six factories, viz. Chinsura, Cassimbazar, Balasore, Patna, Dacca and Malda [6]. Before 1740 the Dutch had "traded" in Bengal for about a century, "brought over countless treasures and transported most vast quantities of commodities"[7].

The territorial property of the Dutch in Bengal was confined to Chinsura and Baranagore [8], which had been "obtained by gift or rather by possession" [9] from the Nawab's government. Their Council at Chinsura was for all purposes subordinate to the authority of the Government at Batavia [10]. All vacancies in it were filled up from Batavia, and it could only appoint members 'ad interim'. Sometimes, however, orders and letters were received by the Dutch Council at Chinsura direct from Holland, replies to which were also sent there. The government at Chinsura consisted of a Director and seven members, five of whom had 'concluding voices' and the other two could 'advise but not vote'. There were chiefs of the factories at Cassimbazar, Patna, and some other places. The Director was obliged "by his instructions to

1. Tavernier, Travels in India, ediied by Ball, p. 122.
2. John Marshall in India, edited by Shaafat Ahmad Khan, p. 101.
3. Ibid, p. 65.
4. Ibid, p. 113.
5. The Diaries of Streynsham Master, edited by Sir Richard Carnac Temple, Vol. I, p. 365.
6. Ibid, Vol. II, p. 92.
7. S. C. Hill, Bengal in 1756-57, Vol. I, p. 29.
8. Stavorinus, Voyage to the East Indies, Vol. I, p. 512.
9. Ibid.
10. Ibid, pp. 502-12.

submit all matters,....of any importance to the Council and to come to a conclusion on the subject by a majority of votes". But it seldom happened that a resolution contrary to his inclination was adopted by the Council, for all members were dependent upon him, "with respect to the profits of their offices". He received large emoluments, for besides a certain percentage allowed to him on the sale of all goods which were imported[1], there were "numerous other means of accumulating money, especially by his having large sums at his disposal, and being consequently enabled to make an immense profit by the employment thereof". The Director alone enjoyed the privilege of being carried in a palanquin 'fitting upon a chair'. Military honours were shown to him at the gate of the fort and he was always attended in his journey by many *chobdars*[2], peons, and other servants. The second in position to the Director was the chief of the factory at Kalikapur near Cassimbazar, who had the rank of a senior merchant. The Dutch Company's Resident in the mint at Murshidabad was under his control. The third in rank in the Council was the chief administrator, who had equally the rank of a senior merchant, and was treated with the same respect as the Chief at Kalikapur. All affairs relating to commerce and the warehouses were entrusted to this officer, subject to the superior control of the Director. One member of the Council was Superintendent of the cloth-room, where the Company's piecegoods were examined, sorted, and despatched. The Superintendent had under him a second with the rank of a junior merchant, three book-keepers or assistants who had to look after the packing of goods, and some *banians*[3] who

1. "Five percent upon the sale of goods imported, is divided, two-thirds to the Director, and one-third to the Second in command; and five percent is allowed to the purchase of opium, and divided two-fifths to the Director, one-fifth to the chief administrator, three-tenths to the chief at Patna, and one-tenth to the second in command there". Stavorinus, op. cit., Vol. I, p, 503, footnote.

2. An attendant carrying short staff or mace. A staff-bearer. "An attendent on a man of rank, one of whose employments is to announce the approach of visitors. He waits with a long staff plated with silver, and runs before his master proclaiming aloud his titles."

3. A Hindu shopkeeper or merchant. A Hindu assistant "employed in the management of commercial affairs". Bolts describes a banian as a

rendered many useful services. The Captain or Chief of the military was also a member of the Council, but he had no vote and could only express his opinion. He had the rank of a senior merchant and he was next to the chief administrator in position. The fiscal or sheriff, who was at the same time Mayor of the town of Chinsura, had the rank of a senior merchant as long as he was in that station, though he had only the pay and allowance of a junior merchant. As a sheriff, it was his duty to see that the Company's interests did not suffer on account of the private trade of its servants; and, as a Mayor, he decided all minor disputes among the Indians living within the Company's limits. The controller of equipments had also a seat in the Council but like the military commander he could only deliver his opinion and had no vote. The Council had a Secretary, who was generally at the same time cashier. Besides this "Civil Council" there was a "Council of Justice", composed of some junior merchants and two military officers with the head administrator as its President. This Council could pass sentences of death subject to the confirmation of the Government at Batavia, but the Nawab's Government did not allow the execution of those sentences "except within the walls of the Company's lodge, or on board of their ships."

Commercial Competition

French trade in Bengal began to decline considerably since the forties of the eighteenth century owing to lack of funds and incompetence of the successors of Dupleix, who, after a successful career as Intendant of Chandernagore, had been transferred to Pondichery in 1741, and it was almost ruined as a sequel to French reverses in Bengal in 1757. But the Dutch had then "great trading interest" in the province. They claimed the 'premier rank' among the Europeans at the Murshidabad *darbar*[1] and the 'precedence of laying and removing the buoys at

---

person "by whom the English gentlemen in Bengal transact all their business. He is interpreter, head-book-keeper, head Secretary, head-broker, the supplier of cash and cash-keeper, and in general also secret-keeper".

1. Hill, Bengal in 1756-57, Vol. II, p. 257.

their pleasure' in the Hugli river[1]. The Dutch were, in fact, the principal commercial rival of the English in this province even during the decades from 1740. Naturally there was keen competition between them in the matter of procuring suitable articles of export from the different manufacturing centres. In 1739 the members of the English factory at Patna had a bitter dispute with those of the Dutch factory in this city regarding saltpetre "bought jointly which was seized by the Dutch with an armed force". As matters grew serious, the Council in Calcutta complained about them to the Dutch Council at Hugli, whereupon an amicable settlement was effected by the month of June of that year[2]. Again, in the year 1741 the Chief of the Dutch factory at Patna, "contrary to an agreement endeavoured to procure all the saltpetre he could to the (English) Company's Prejudice"[3]. The Council in Calcutta complained against it to the Dutch Director at Hugli, who "promised to write strenuously to Patna". In March 1744 Mr. Barwell, Mr. Guillander and Mr. Drabbe, Chiefs of the English, French and Dutch factories respectively at Patna, in consideration of "common interest of the three Nations", particularly in order to "bring over the merchants to reasonable terms", entered into a contract regarding saltpetre trade in Bihar[4]. It was stipulated thereby that in the said year, Mr. Drabbe "alone shall buy up all the saltpetre", that the English and the French or their agents shall not "buy saltpetre at any place or under any pretext whatsoever, nor shall they receive any into their Factories or other places dependent on them", and that the Dutch Chief shall deliver to the other Companies their respective shares of Dobara saltpetre at the rate of Sicca rupees three and four annas per maund. But in the next year Omichand and Deepchand, two influential merchants, "offered at Durbar (the Nawab's *darbar*) Rs. 25,000 to oblige Europeans to buy (saltpetre) solely of them"[5]. At this, the three European Companies entered into another contract on the 8th January,

1. Ibid, p. 287.
2. Letter to Court, 3rd January, 1740, para 86.
3. Letter to Court, 11th December, 1741, para 218.
4. Vide Appendix 'A'.
5. Letter to Court, 31st January, 1746, paras 47-59.

1746, for the purchase of saltpetre, the principal terms[1] of it being almost similar to those of the contract of the year 1744. The chiefs of the three Companies at Patna agreed in April, 1746, to "hold this contract as good and valid". But fulfilment of this contract was prevented by certain factors, and co-operation between the Dutch and the English regarding saltpetre trade in Bihar disappeared in the course of the next year[2]. In 1753 the English made a contract with Omichand for the provision of saltpetre, the demand for which as the principal ingredient in the manufacture of gunpowder had been gradually growing among the Europeans because of their wars. In 1758 Clive secured absolute control of the English East India Company over the saltpetre farms in Bihar from their puppet, Nawab Mir Jafar.

Political Relations

Besides commercial interests, other factors, Indian as well as extra-Indian, then greatly influenced the policies of, and relations among, the respective European trading Companies in India. Various evils were, like deadly cankers, then eating into the vitality of Indian life in all its phases. Gradual disappearance of political unity, sound governance and administrative order, the unpatriotic and selfish policies of a debased aristocracy, growing lack of progressive and inspiring ideals in society as well as literature, and rapid economic decline, doomed India to a pathetic state of alround insolvency. This, indeed, whetted the political ambitions of the European trading nations in India and made their penetration into her politics quicker, bolder, and deeper than before[3]. Further, the international rivalries and complications among the European powers, in the widely scattered regions of the globe, since the forties of the eighteenth century had also a large share in reshaping the political destiny

1. Vide Appendix 'B'.
2. Vide K. K. Datta, Bengal Subah, Vol. I, pp. 373-80.
3. The beginnings of European penetration into the sphere of Indian politics can be traced earlier. The mid-eighteenth century political disturbances in India served to accelerate it.

of India. Voltaire aptly observed : "the first canon shot fired in our lands was to set the match to all the batteries in America and in Asia". The War of the Austrian succession, the Seven Years' War, the War of American Independence, and the Revolutionary and Napoleonic Wars, had profound repercussions on the history of India during the critical years of the eighteenth century and the early nineteenth century. In fact, India, then internally bankrupt in all respects and coveted as respective spheres of influence by the rival European nations like the English, the French, and the Dutch, became one of the theatres of their hostilities, destined to produce momentous consequences in world history.

Thus, when the echo of the War of Austrian Succession reached here, southern India was terribly convulsed on account of the imperialistic ambitions and military exploits of the French and the English. But Bengal was then saved from the ravages of war owing to proper vigilance and timely precautions on the part of its tactful Nawab Alivardi. He not only tried to control effectively the trade of the Europeans in his *subah*, but was also determined to prevent the extension there of political influence by any of them. "He saw with indignation and surprise," remarks M. Jean Law, "the progress of the French and the English nations on the Coromandal coast as well as in the Deccan, for by means of spies he was informed of everything that happened there....He feared that sooner or later the Europeans would attempt similar enterprises in his government"[1]. He very wisely pursued a policy of neutrality during the Deccan wars and turned a deaf ear to the request of the French commander, Bussy, for his alliance against the English[2]. In order to enforce this policy of neutrality on the Europeans in Bengal, he issued a *parwanah* in July, 1745, forbidding the English, the French and the Dutch to commit "any hostilities against each other in his dominions"[3]. Point Palmyras[4] was

1. S. C. Hill, Bengal in 1756-57, Vol. III, pp. 160-61.
2. Siyar ul-mutakherin, Vol. II, pp. 45-46.
3. Correspondance du Conseil de Chandernagor avec divers, 2e partie, p. 350; K. K. Datta, Alivardi and his Times, pp. 155-159
4. A promontory and a small town on the coast of the Bay of Bengal to the south of Balasore.

fixed as the place from where neutrality was to be observed.

This strong policy of the Nawab prevented the European traders from converting Bengal into a scene of active conflicts among themselves during his regime. But they kept themselves prepared for emergencies and once actually violated the neutrality of the Ganges. Subject to French aggressions, Holland turned to be an ally of England in the course of the war of Austrian Succession. This Anglo-Dutch alliance against the French was sought to be made effective in India also. The merchants of the Dutch Company were given the liberty to "trade anywhere on English territory"[1] and the Dutch at Cochin passed orders to all the captains of their vessels "to keep themselves ready for action"[2]. In April, 1748, Galenus Mersen, the Dutch Governor of Negapatam, wrote to the English Council at Fort St. David : "Our high superiors at Batavia have resolved in consequence of the hostilities that have been committed by the Crown of France upon the territories and places of our sovereign in the Netherlands without declaring war, to repel force by force and to do that nation all possible damage in these ports by sea and land, and have likewise strenuously commanded us and the ministers of the Governments and Settlements belonging to our Company not only to break off all correspondence and traffic with that nation, but also to prevent the least help or assistance from being given to them even in the most indifferent matters, and, on the contrary, to entertain the strictest correspondence with you and your nation as our allies that the mutual preservation of both requires, and in case of need to afford you all the assistance in our power to intimidate our common enemy and ward off the blows which they intend us. We shall punctually fulfil and obey that order"[3]. The Council at Fort St. David forwarded this letter to the Council in Calcutta on the 21st April, 1748[4]. Some Dutch deputies from Hugli also attended the Council in Calcutta "to acquaint the Governor of the orders of their superiors prohibiting all

1. A Dutch letter from Cochin, dated 29th September, 1747 (Madras Government Records).
2. Ibid, dated 13th November, 1747.
3. Bengal Consultations, 16th May, 1748.
4. Letter to Court, 19th November, 1748, para. 120.

manner of intercourse between their settlement and that of Chandernagore" and also of the orders "given to their pilots to be cautious how they trust to colours, and on no account whatever to give any assistance to the French"[1].

After a French squadron, commanded by M. Bouvet[2], Governor of the Isle of Bourbon, had appeared off Negapatam on the 9th June, 1748, and the Calcutta Council had been informed of it in a few days by Commander Griffin and Captain Parker, the Dutch at Hugli promised their assistance to the English[3]. In reply to a letter from Mr. Barwell[4], the English Governor in Calcutta, Mr. Huyghens, the Dutch Director at Chinsura, observed that the Dutch Council had issued necessary "orders to bring their Company's ship up to Baranagore to be unloaded, from whence they will order her down to Calcutta to assist" the English in case the French attacked that place, and that they were prepared to pass further orders for "all their expected Company's ship to be brought to Baranagore as soon as they come into the river" (Hugli), on the English Company giving him sufficient assurance that they would not admit into their service, or grant shelter to, any of the sailors or others on board the ships sent to help them but would deliver them up on demand[5]. Shortly after this, an unfortunate incident was about to disturb this alliance. A Dutch vessel, sent to carry three indisposed sailors from one of the Dutch ships lying off Fulta, was attacked, just below Calcutta, by some armed sailors from an English ship which lay at anchor there. They took away three sailors, one of them being George Jansen of Dutch nationality, and assaulted a *majhi* (helmsman) and a peon in

1. Bengal Consultations, 30th May, 1748.

2. Orme, History of the Military Transactions of the British Nation in Indostan, Vol. II, p. 92.

3. Letter to Court, 29th November, 1748, para. 122.

4. Mr. Forster, Governor of Calcutta, died in March, 1748. Mr. John Jackson, who had been appointed his successor, also died on the 20th March. So Mr. William Barwell, who was next in position, took charge of the government of Calcutta on the 18th April, 1748. Wilson, Fort William in Bengal, Vol. I, p. 201, footnote. For a sketch of Mr. Barwell's career by Sir William Foster vide Bengal: Past and Present, January-June, 1924, pp. 35-43.

5. Bengal Consultations, July, 1748.

such a way that the "latter fell overboard and in all appearance went down the water and the former died there of his wounds". Mr. Huyghens thereupon wrote to the Council in Calcutta that the English Company should give to the Netherlands Company, "whose colour has been scandalised by the violence committed, a due satisfaction (which they hereby demand) by ordering the malefactors to be punished in a most severe manner, that others may be terrified and constrained from undertaking the like, and any other violence against their boats". He also demanded that George Jansen, and another named Hordonk, who had left the Dutch vessel, Cost Capelle, on the 25th August 1745, and were then in the English Company's military service, should be delivered to him. To prevent an open rupture with the Dutch at that critical time, the Council in Calcutta satisfied most of his demands[1].

Towards the end of year 1748, the French forcibly occupied the Dutch Company's garden of Champonade[2]. Mr. Huyghens immediately informed Mr. Barwell of this action on the part of the French, which, in his opinion, was against the principle of neutrality[3]. At this the Council in Calcutta authorised the President to report to the Nawab in a petition that the French had violated "the neutrality of the Ganges" which made them reasonably apprehend aggression on their part on themselves[4]. Mr. Huyghens also wrote a letter of remonstrance to M. Renault, the French Chief at Chandernagore, on the 13th January, 1749, against this agressive behaviour of the French men[5]. The French Chief sent a reply to him to the following effect :—"Permit us to tell you that your protests do not appear to us well-founded. It is you gentlemen who were the first to have violated the neutrality by breaking with us all communication, a procedure which ought to have caused us all the more

1. Consultations, September, 1748.

2. Bengal Consultations, 3rd January, 1749. This garden was "in the centre of Fort Gustavas having three terraces, one rising above the other, ornamented with flowers." Long, Selections from Unpublished Records of the Government of India, Vol. I. p. 15, footnote.

3. Consultations, 3rd January, 1749.

4. Ibid.

5. Correspondence du Conseil de Chandernagore aver divers, 2e. partie, p. 371.

astonishment, as intercourse between our two establishments has never been interrupted even in times of war. The step which we have just taken is only too well justified by your conduct and by the situation of your garden so near our fortifications as to obstruct our passage. Moreover, the little space, which hemmed in our colony and which does not contain even an acre of land, ought to interest your nation less than the buildings which are there and which have been raised up at the expense of Mr. Sichterman (1744 A. D.) as centre door"[1]. It was only a few months after the cessation of hostilities in Europe that the garden of the Dutch was restored to them in April, 1749[2].

Dutch Trade

During this period the trade of the Dutch in Bengal was sometimes disturbed by local troubles. In January 1748 Shamshir Khan, leader of the Afghan insurrection of that year against Alivardi's government, demanded "a General Tax from the 3 European Factorys (factories— the English, the Dutch and the French) of 40 or 50,000 Rupees"[3] and his followers plundered the Dutch factory at Futwah "of white cloth and other goods to the amount of 65,000 Rupees"[4]. The repeated Maratha inroads into Bengal must have also caused occasional inconvenience to the Dutch.

But, on the whole, the prospects of Dutch trade in Bengal were then encouraging. Nawab Alivardi was quite particular about exerting his political authority over the European nations in Bengal and controlling their trade, but he did not injure it in any way[5]. Mr. Bisdom, the Dutch chief at Chinsura,

---

1. Ibid.

2. Ibid: The Treaty of Aix-la-Chapelle was signed by England, France, and Holland on the 16th October 1748. Spain agreed to it on the 20th October, Austria on the 8th, and Sardinia on the 20th November. The news of this Treaty reached India about a couple of months later (Bengal Letter to Court, dated 27th January, 1749, para 1).

3. Letter to Court, 19th November, 1748, paras 56 & 81.

4. Ibid, para. 81 and Consultations, 8th March, 1748.

5. Vide K. K. Datta, Alivardi and His Times, Chapter V.

mentioned in his petition to Siraj-ud-daulah, dated the 26th June, 1756, that in the past they had "generally been befriended and countenanced by the Princes of the land and, up to the glorious Nawab Souja-ul-mulk-Mahabat Jung (Alivardi) inclusive, always endowed with privileges"[1]. In 1730 Nawab Shuja-ud-din had issued a *parwanah*[2] in their favour, reiterating thereby in strong terms the privileges granted to them by some old *firmans*, which had by that time ceased to be effective on account of the disorders and confusion prevailing in the country since the early years of the eighteenth century. This *parwanah* contained "strictest injunctions" against all kinds of "molestation" and impediments which prejudiced their trade in any way. In 1748 Nawab Alivardi issued a *parwanah*[3] directing the officers of the *Buxbundar*[4] at Hugli to collect customs from the Dutch private merchants at the same rate like that of the Dutch Company, that is, 2½ per cent, instead of 3½ per cent, which the former had been required to pay so long.

As has been already noted, the Dutch had to reckon with the keen competition of the English Company. Their commercial jealousy did not disappear because of their temporary diplomatic alliance. In 1746 the Dutch in India claimed an exclusive right of trade in opium. The English East India Company could not submit to it. Even before the War of the Austrian Succession came to a close, the Court of Directors in England had sent positive orders[5] to the Company's officers in India to oppose this pretension of the Dutch by all means. The Council in Calcutta wrote to the Court of Directors on the 24th February, 1749 : "We have directed your Honour's Orders in relation to the Dutch Pretences to an exclusive Trade in opium to be affixed at the Public places in our Town and shall acquaint all the commanders of ships to act agreeable to your Directions". In 1752 an English prisoner "escaped" the bounds of Calcutta and placed himself under "the protection of the Dutch flag" at

1. Hill, op. cit., Vol. I, p. 29.
2. Vide Appendix 'C',
3. Vide Appendix 'D'.
4. Customs-office at Hugli.
5. Monumental Remains of the Dutch East India Company by Alexr. Rea, p. 24.

Baranagore[1]. In their letter to Bengal, dated 31st January, 1755, the Court of Directors complained that the English Company's servants were supplying their "Dutch rivals" with goods to the great prejudice of their masters' trade.

Occasional co-operation among the European Companies.

Occasionally, however, the English, the French and the Dutch companies in Bengal acted in concert to prevent their common interests being prejudiced in any way. In 1751 the Nawab's government passed an order on the three European companies "to send all money whether Bullion or Rupees to the Mint at Muxadavad (Murshidabad) to be coined there into Siccas or disposed of to Jugutseat (Jagat Seth) and forbidding the Europeans to pay away any Money to their Merchants but in new Siccas" [2]. Considering that this measure would prove to be of the "utmost ill consequence" [3] to the Company's trade, the Council in Calcutta instructed the gentlemen of the Cassimbazar factory "to act in concert with the French and Dutch" [4]. The Chief of the factories of the three Companies at Cassimbazar decided to present separately "an Arsdatt (petition) to the Nobob (Nawab) setting forth the hardships (their) respective Companies would (thereby) suffer and requesting that Bullion and Rupees might pass as usual" [5]. This step produced "the desired effect" [6]. When a vessel, under the protection of a Prussian Company, started in 1753 for trading in the East, was ready to proceed from Emden to India, the Court of Directors in England communicated the following instructions to the Council: ...."You may be well on your guard to prevent any Encroachment upon our Rights and Privileges and that the Agents of the said Company may not meet with encouragement from any Persons whatsoever under our Protection. You are to

1. Letter to Court, 17th February, 1752, para. 7.
2. Ibid, para. 2.
3. Ibid, para. 79.
4. Letter to Court, 18th September, 1752, para. 79.
5. Ibid.
6. Ibid, Court's Letter to Bengal, 23rd January, 1754, para. 57.

give positive orders to all our Pylots not to take charge of the said ship or the ships belonging to any other Powers, who are not established in India to bring them up the river and you are to endeavour to induce the Agents of the French and Dutch Companies to do the same; and you are likewise to use your endeavours in concert with the French and Dutch Agents to prevent the Prussians getting possession of the late Ostend Factory at Hughly or making any other Settlement in Bengal"[1]. In reply the Council in Calcutta informed the Court on the 6th September, 1754, that they had obeyed their orders punctually, that the French and the Dutch had given favourable answers and that "nothing shall be wanting" on their part "to put every obstacle" they "can devise in their way"[2]. About the month of July, 1755, Mir. Abu Taleb, *naib* of Krishnadas, "on a pretence of a demand of some considerable present from the Dutch Factory there, had seized a writer belonging to the Dutch and confined him in the Kellah (fort) till the Dutch Chief (Mr. Tsinck) made a promise of complying with their demand"[3]. Considering it to be "a most virulent and unprecedented proceeding to an European", the three European Companies proposed to send a joint appeal to the Nawab at Murshidabad[4].

---

1. Court's Letter to Bengal, 23rd January, 1754, para. 106.
2. Para. 11.
3. Consultations, 14th July, 1755.
4. Ibid.

CHAPTER II

The Critical Months of 1756-57

Relations with the Nawab

The months of 1756-57 formed indeed a crucial point in the history of Bengal. Events were then moving there with the flickering quickness of a cinematograph film to culminate in a weighty revolution. The quarrel between its Nawab, Siraj-ud-daulah, and the English East India Company, attended with so many deadly evils, naturally created serious problems for all connected with Bengal in any way whatsoever. They had to watch its course with deep anxiety and suspense, and Fate ultimately decreed in favour of the English on the 23rd June, 1757. Open hostility of the French against the English resulted in the virtual eclipse of the former's influence in Bengal in 1757. The Dutch, even without any active participation in the conflicts of the time, found themselves placed in an extremely critical situation.

Siraj-ud-daulah sought to utilise the services of the Dutch, the French and the Danes in Bengal in his anti-English enterprises. He at first drew *parwanas* for the three companies assuring them therein of his favour. On the 26th May, 1756, he wrote to Khawjah Wajid from Rajmahal to deliver these to them and to "endeavour to engage these nations to prevent the English resettling themselves", after they had been driven out [1]. Before marching towards Calcutta, the Nawab summoned the native agents of the French and the Dutch at Cassimbazar to his *darbar* with a view to ascertaining from them what sort of assistance he might expect from their respective masters in his meditated expedition against the English. The Dutch agent instantly replied that his "Company was only mercantile, not constituted for making war, and that at Chinsura there were not more than 10 guns and 50 soldiers including both whites and blacks" [2]. But on his way to Calcutta the Nawab sent *parwa-*

---

1. S. C. Hill, Bengal in 1756-57 Vol. I, p. 3.
2. Ibid, p. 21.

nas to the Dutch, the French and the Danes "to be expeditious in getting their vessels of force in readiness to accompany" his "land army and attack the English by the river while he besieged them on shore"[1].

The Dutch did not evidently comply with the Nawab's demand, which had the effect of highly exasperating him against them. On the 22nd June, 1756, he sent the following *parawana* to Adrian Bisdom, the Dutch Director : "I have too frequently written to you from Moorshedabad that you were to join your power to the King's army for the destruction of the wicked English by water, though your not doing so is of no account whatever and you were asked only to put you to the test, for by God's blessing and help I am so strongly provided that I find myself able to exterminate ten such nations as these English, and if you wish to ensure the continuation of the Company's trade in this country, you will have to act in accordance with what I caused to be made known to you through my friend Faggeruttojjar Coja (Khawjah) Mhameth Wajid[2]; but in the contrary case, it will be all over with your trade in the soubaship, which is a true warning concerning which you must know your own mind"[3]. On receipt of this "definite sentence,"[4] the Dutch Director, accompanied by d' Armenault and Tsinck, called on Khawjah Wajid in the afternoon of the 24th June, 1756, "to enquire as to the real purport of" the Nawab's desire. Khawjah Wajid informed him that the Nawab had been highly displeased with the Dutch for their refusal to assist in the matter of expelling the English out of Bengal, and had expressed the following before him at the time of his (Khawjah Wajid's) departure from his *darbar*: "Tell the Hollanders, they must bring me twenty lacs of rupees or I will ruin them as I have done the English"[5]. In fact, the Nawab after reaching Hugli on the 25th June, 1756[6], on his way back from Calcutta to Murshi-

1. Ibid, p. 5.
2. An Armenian and "the principal merchant of the province, who resided at Hugli". Fakhr-ul-Tujjar—Chief of Merchants.
3. Hill, op. cit., Vol. I, p. 26.
4. Ibid.
5. Ibid, p. 27.
6. Ibid, p. 33.

dabad, demanded 20 lacs of rupees from the Dutch Director, Mr. Bisdom. After due deliberation, the Dutch Director decided that there was no alternative but to take Khawjah Wajid "in hand and under promise of gratuity to request him to use his powerful influence, in order, if possible, to satisfy the Prince with an ordinary Nazrani (*Nazarana*) or at least with mediocre contribution". He made such a request to Khawjah Wajid, who, thereupon, assured him of his friendship, and promised to get hold of a favourable moment to intercede with the Nawab for the Dutch. The Dutch Council at Hugli unanimously approved of this procedure on the part of their Director in their general meeting on Friday, the 25th June, 1756, and further resolved "to make shift and bear the cost of freight for the boats to transfer the army, but for the rest not to agree to the Nawab's demand, unless susceptible of great reduction, as being altogether under constraint"[1].

Khawjah Wajid waited upon the Nawab in the evening of the 25th June, at an opportune moment, and pleaded so strongly for the Dutch that he authorised Khawjah Wajid, Rajah Durlabbram[2] and a few of his other trusted courtiers to fix the amount to be paid by the Dutch asking them at the same time "to bear in mind that he had been put to heavy expenses and had to bear still more". The mediators immediately decided that the Dutch should pay 4 lacs of rupees to the Nawab and half a lac to them as a reward for their intercession.

The Dutch considered this amount to be rather exorbitant. But as matters stood, there was no other way left for them than to satisfy the Nawab as soon as possible. He had sent his Master of Requests, in the morning of the 26th of June, 1756, to demand the delivery of Dutch artillery and flags and had already besieged the Dutch settlement at Hugli, whose inhabitants had fled before 70,000 armed men equipped with better artillery and all kinds of war ammunition. The Dutch force at Hugli was a poor match for the besiegers. The Dutch felt that any attempt on their part to oppose the Nawab's army might vitally affect their own interests. They apprehended that because of this their

---

1. Ibid, p. 27.
2. Vide my article on Durlabhram in Indian Historical Quarterly, 1940.

"servants at Cassimbazar, Patna, and elsewhere would be exposed to the fury" of the Nawab and the Dutch Company's assets in the respective factories and in the Mint, as well as those deposited at the quarters (*aurungs ?*) and the money in circulation to the amount of about 46 lacs of rupees (or 70 tons of treasure) would be lost in such a case, not to mention that if things turned out adversely....honour would be impaired,....credit broken and probably not fifty lacs of rupees would suffice to make good the damage done to the Company....''[1].

In this extreme situation, the Dutch Council decided to try for a reduction of these heavy demands of the Nawab by sending him an appeal in the following terms : "Renowned Prince. The Hollanders have traded here for a century and a half, have brought over countless treasures and transported most vast quantities of commodities, under prompt payment of tolls and dues, wherefore they have generally been befriended and countenanced especially by the princes of the land and up to the glorious Nawab Souja-ul-Molk Mahabat Jung inclusive, always endowed with privileges. They have always been faithful to their benefactors, and if even guilty of a wrongful act they were never backward in granting satisfaction. And yet it has pleased Your Highness to exact a contribution from us much heavier than we are able to pay, considering the calamities that have befallen us on sea and many losses we have of of late years encountered in our commercial transactions, wherefore I do humbly beseech your Excellency to confer the great favour upon us of graciously treating us with reasonable moderation in reference to the *nazarani* (*nazarana*). May your Highness's power and glory go on increasing"[2]. The Company's *vakil* was charged with the task of handing over the missive to the mediators for delivering it to the Nawab, and he was also invested with the power of attorney "to make a bid in respect of the contribution demanded" provided it did not "exceed the sum of two lacs of rupees, besides the expenses"[3]. But when

1. Hill, op. cit., Vol. I, 29.
2. Ibid, pp. 29-30. Nazarana — "A ceremonial present or offering to a superior".

Aurang— A place where goods were "manufactured or produced for sale; for a depot for such goods."

3. Hill, op. cit., Vol. I, p. 30.

the Dutch *vakil* appeared before Khawjah Wajid and the other mediators, the latter refused to deliver that petition to the Nawab, and expressed that they would "wash their hands of the business leaving the issue to the responsibility of the Dutch"[1]. Apprehending early reprisals from the Nawab's side, the Dutch Council unanimously resolved in the evening of the 26th June, 1756, to pay the Nawab the sum of four hundred thousand sicca rupees "by written bond (on account of scarcity of cash) payable three months after date"[2]. They further decided that at first they would forward 10,000 sicca rupees in cash to Khawjah Wajid in order to satisfy the mediators and would also request the Nawab "to grant a sanad or general order for the free and uninterrupted carrying on of the Company's commercial dealings everywhere, etc., and the confirmation of its privileges"[3].

But this did not satisfy the Nawab. Next morning, Khawjah Wajid's *gomasta* brought back to the Dutch at Hugli the bond for 400,000 sicca rupees, issued in favour of the Nawab. He was accompanied by Bajenaat (Baijnath), an agent of the Murshidabad bankers, Jagat Seths, because the Nawab being in immediate need of fund desired that, if the Dutch were not in a position to pay him in cash they should negotiate with Bajenaat to borrow the amount from his masters[4] who often lent money to the European traders in Bengal. Considering the inadvisability of incurring the Nawab's displeasure, the Dutch agreed to conform to his desire. The bond in favour of the Nawab was withdrawn and a new one, with interest at the ordinary rate of 3/4 per cent a month, was executed in favour of the Jagat Seths[5]. Further, according to the Nawab's suggestion, the Director and the Head Administrator went to him "to render due salutation"[6].

1. Ibid.
2. Ibid, p. 31.
3. Ibid.
4. Ibid, p. 32.
5. "We the undersigned acting on behalf of and for the account of the General Netherlands East India Company do hereby acknowledge having effected a loan of four hundred thousand sicca rupees with the bill-brokers Jagat Seth, Fettusjentie and Seth Amendjendie, which, sum together with the interest due thereon at the rate of 9 percent per annum, or 3/4 per cent a month, we promise to pay when the service of the East India Company shall allow of its being done." Ibid, I, 32.
6. Ibid, pp. 33-34.

Being received by him in a friendly manner, they were presented with robes of honour, a head-dress set with precious stones, an elephant and a horse. They were also assured by the Nawab that he "would see to the necessary *parwanas* for the confirmation of the Company's privileges on his arrival at Murshidabad"[1]. The Nawab returned to his capital on the 11th July, 1756.

The wheel of politics took a new turn in Bengal in the course of a few months. Through the efforts of Watson and Clive the English East India Company recovered their lost settlement of Calcutta by the 3rd of January, 1757, and captured the Fort at Hugli within a few days. With consequent restoration of their influence they found themselves in such a position of advantage as emboldened them to manifest a defiant attitude towards the Nawab and even to extort his consent to some of their demands. Admiral Watson wrote to the Nawab, on the 6th February, 1757 : "If you are wise, you will grant them the justice that is their due; otherwise, the sword is going to be drawn that will never be sheathed again"[2]. Various adverse circumstances forced the Nawab to conclude a treaty[3] with the English East India Company on the 9th February, 1757. The material and moral effects of this treaty were indeed very significant. Its terms were highly favourable to the commercial and political interests of the English in Bengal, and they immediately enhanced their prestige. Edward Ives significantly observes : "Thus by the spirited and gallant behaviour of two English Commanders, the affairs of the Company which a few months before seemed verging on inevitable ruin, were not only quite retrieved but put upon a firmer and better footing than ever....the treaty was honourable, and advantageous for us...."[4]. The Nawab's prestige and influence were certainly damaged to a great extent. In fact, he began henceforth to live "by the light of a star" that had paled, and signs of disaffection and treachery appeared among many of his soldiers and officers, including Mir Jafar[5].

1. Ibid, p. 55.
2. Ives' Voyage, p. 113.
3. Ibid, pp. 113-16.
4. Ibid, p. 118.
5. Scrafton, Reflections on the Government of Indostan, p. 66.

The Dutch at Cassimbazar considered this to be a convenient opportunity to take a bold stand in their relation with the Nawab. Mr. Vernet, Chief of the Dutch Factory there, observed in his letter to the Dutch Director at Chinsura, dated the 28th February, 1757: "....It is more necessary in these countries than elsewhere and especially in these times to uphold the prestige of the Company as much as possible, and also that more is to be got now from the Nawab—he being stricken with great fear of the Europeans—by haughty than by a submissive behaviour"[1]. The Dutch Council at Cassimbazar then sent an *arzi* (petition) of their Director to the Nawab through their *vakil* instead of through the Second of the Council. But the Dutch *vakil* was put to disgrace for this underestimation of the Nawab's power by his masters. No sooner had the *arzi* been presented to the Nawab "than he grew very angry and gave vent to much abusive language asking the *vakil* whether the Dutch were playing the fool with him, at the same time ordering him to be pinioned and to have him shambocked." He was saved of this humiliation through the intervention of Durlabhram and Jagat Seth, but was locked up in the *Munshikhana* till the evening when the Nawab sent him a *parawana* with order to bring a speedy reply to it from the Chief of the Dutch Factory at Cassimbazar. He also sent a gold-stick-bearer to the said Chief to let him know that he had torn their Director's *arzi* into pieces. Jagat Seth and Rajah Durlabhram pleaded much in favour of the Dutch but to no effect[2].

The Nawab, however, seems to have been pacified within a few days, and came to be favourably disposed towards the Dutch. The Dutch Director at Hugli accordingly instructed Mr. Vernet on the 13th March to utilise that favourable disposition of the Nawab to further their own interests. "To strike the iron while it is hot," he observed, "we hereby commission you either direct or through the intermediary of persons whom you may trust, to enter into negotiations with him in order to add stress to the demands, made by us, for the furtherance of which you may waive out the spent Madrasa (Madras) money to the amount of

1. Hill, op. cit., Vol. II, pp. 257-58.
2. Ibid, pp. 275-77.

40,000 florins, and as for the promise of assistance, we will use our utmost interest with their worships (i. e., the Council General in Batavia) to be enabled to do so, and if we succeed therein, we shall not be disinclined to assist His Excellency against all public enemies of the country, but not against those European nations with which our State is living in peace and amity" [1]. Mr. Vernet was further advised on the 16th March to draw the Nawab's attention to the inconvenience that the Dutch at Hugli suffered from the unfavourable site of their residence, and to request him to grant them a different one pointing it out to him that the French at Chandernagore, then besieged by the English, had sunk some vessels in the river below their fort and had thus blocked the passage from thence to the sea [2].

But some fresh complications soon greatly disconcerted the Nawab. The capture of Chandernagore by the English, which dealt "an unexpressible blow to the French Company", as Clive justly observed, and immensely added to the power and prestige of the victors, could not but cause anxiety in the Nawab's mind. Further, the relations between him and his military officers, particularly Mir Jafar, grew more strained [3]. This made him "so sullen and gloomy" that no one dared approach him with any request [4]. So it did not become possible for the Dutch to put forward their 'solicitations' before him. Mohanlal and Jagat Seth assured them that they would get hold of a 'favourable opportunity' to secure the Nawab's consent to their demands. But that opportune moment was not to come. The conspiracy, which totally undermined the Nawab's position, was already in being [5], and in no time he found himself confronted with an array of hostile influences. The logic of events was irresistibly driving him to the fate of Plassey. In view of all this the Dutch Director advised M. Vernet not to spend any amount for the purpose of "insuring their success of the solicita-

---

1. Ibid, pp. 284-285.
2. Ibid, p. 287.
3. Stewart, History of Bengal, p. 391;
   Hill, op. cit., Vol. II, pp. 410-11.
4. Ibid.
5. Ibid, p. 413.

tions" but "to wait a little and see what turn affairs will take"[1].

Relations with The English

Not only in their relations with the Nawab but also in those with the English East India Company for about a year on the eve of Plassey, the Dutch in Bengal had to act with great caution and prudence. When after storming the English Factory at Cassimbazar, Siraj-ud-daulah commenced his march on the 5th June, 1756, for the attack of Calcutta, the English in Calcutta appealed to the Dutch at Chinsura for help against the Nawab. The former argued that they were entitled to receive it according to the terms of the treaty subsisting between the Governments of England and the Netherlands. "····we have, therefore, considered it our duty to point out to your Honour and the Council," wrote the President of the Council in Calcutta to the Dutch Director at Hugli on the 7th June, 1756, "the danger that lies in the allowing such an insult to one of the European nations settled here to pass unheeded, and request for the sake of our King, and by virtue of the treaty of alliance existing between us, that should we be attacked, you will as far possible render us every aid and assistance in your power. We flatter ourselves that you will not fail in this, owing to the friendship between your Honour and our nation, it being to our common interest to prevent all such annoyances. We request you to make us acquainted, as soon as possible, with your decisions in this respect, and how many soldiers, or other aid, we may expect, for the calamitous state of affairs here renders assistance imperatively necessary"[2]. But, on the next day, the Dutch sent a negative reply[3] to the following effect : "We have heard with great regret of the Nawab's intention to attack you, but to assist you as requested in your missive of yesterday lies beyond our power, as your Honours must fain fairly acknowledge, if you consider the uncertainty as to whether Calcutta alone is the goal, also

1. Ibid, p. 414.
2. Ibid, Vol. I, p. 12.
3. Ibid, pp. 14-15.

the bad situation of our fort and the weakness of our force in Bengal, we have to employ native *barkandazes*[1] in all troubles that arise. As whereas your Honours require the assistance referred to in your aforesaid letter, in the name of His Royal Majesty of Great Britain, and especially by virtue of the treaty existing between the two nations as allies, to render you assistance as for as possible in case of need, we have to reply thereto that, leaving alone that the orders of our superiors charge us to remain neutral in all cases that do not concern us, we cannot see that the reasons upon which your Honours rely necessitate that we, who are established here as simple merchants, should on that account be obliged or feel it our duty, to expose ourselves to dangerous troubles from which we are not sure we shall remain exempt, and as little do we gather from the contents of the said treaty (unless there be another from the one we mean, and which is not in our possession) that the assistance we are bound to render to each other in virtue thereof (when we do not know whether there is room for mediation or not) can in this case be rendered without exposing ourselves to the displeasure of our masters."

Greatly disappointed at what the English in Calcutta regarded as the "cool and indifferent" attitude of the Dutch Council, they protested against it in strong terms in a letter dated the 13th June. They wrote therein that "dangerous consequences" were "likely to ensue" from their "holding aloof, during these mutual negotiations, from the protection" of the "goods and possessions" of the English. They gave also a note of warning to the effect that if they still continued "to look on as mere spectators" of their "destruction", they would report their conduct to their own authorities, who, they believed, "will lay the matter before the Parliament of England" for proper redress. They even suggested the formation of a "triple alliance" among the three European Companies in Bengal against the Nawab[2]. But, in reply to this the Dutch Council observed on

1. " A matchlockman, but commonly applied to a man armed with a sword and stick, who acts as door-keeper, watchman, guard or escort".

2. Hill, op. cit, Vol. I, pp. 17-18.

the 16th June that the engagements between Great Britain and their country did not "extend to the colonies here in India", and that, in view of the critical situation in which they had been then placed, their combination with them against the Nawab would be a "perilous undertaking" on their part[1]. They also pleaded that their masters in Holland and at Batavia had prescribed to them "a strict maintenance of neutrality in all cases that relate in any way to the native Government"[2].

The capture of Calcutta by Siraj-ud-daulah within a few days caused immense embarrassment to the English East India Company in Bengal. Mr. Drake, the Governor, and some others, fled away to Fulta, where they were exposed to extreme miseries for want of suitable shelter and provisions. In this period of adversity the English refugees at Fulta sent a heartfelt appeal to the Dutch President in the following terms on the 25th June : "We address this to you from Voltha (Fulta) whither we have been obliged to retire with a few of the inhabitants, who have fled from Calcutta, and being entirely dertitute of any kind of provisions clothing, and of the bare necessaries of life, as also in great want of anchors and cables, etc., for our ships, we beg to express your heartfelt wish that you may favour us with aid and succour in our distress, and help us from Hoogley with all kinds of liquors and clothing, together with anchors, cables and tackle and also give instructions to your officials at Voltha, etc., to assist us as lies in their power, we always being ready to reimburse the value of the same. As we hope that your Government may enjoy tranquillity, we flatter ourselves that, viewing the intimate agreement between the two nations your Honour will not fail to send us information from time to time as to whether there is a possibility of our being able to return in personal safety to Calcutta, as regards which point please put yourself in our position and favour us with the earliest intelligence concerning the purpose of the Nawab and the progress he is making"[3].

The Dutch Council decided on the 28th June "to render the aforesaid fugitives no assistance in the present troublous times and to avoid all correspondence with them, and therefore not to

1. Ibid, pp. 18-19.
2. Ibid.
3. Long, p. 76 ; Hill, op. cit., Vol. I, p. 25.

reply to their aforesaid missives"[1]. They maintained this attitude for a few days more. But on the 20th of July they came to a "secret resolution in consideration of the close alliances" between their nation and the English "to provide the Fulta fugitives with some food and clothes intending to charge it to the English Company and also the anchors, 17 in number, which they had taken from Fulta for their use"[2]. Thus, in spite of the strict orders of the Nawab's Government against helping the English fugitives in any way, the Dutch at Chinsura helped them with provisions and some necessary information[3]. Mr. Holwell writes that "the humanity and friendship" which he and his few companions received from the gentlemen of the Dutch and French factories near Murshidabad, during the days of their confinement in that city in July, 1756, deserved their "most grateful remembrance"[4].

To help a distressed power was no doubt a humanitarian act. But the action of the Dutch in rendering assistance to the Fulta fugitives in a secret manner was not consistent with what they had recently professed or with the laws of neutrality as were then understood in Europe[5]. Strictly speaking, according to the principle of neutrality, a neutral power could not,

---

1. Ibid, p. 38.
2. Ibid, pp. 302–308.
3. Ibid, p. 38 ; Long, p. 76.
4. Holwell's Letter to Richard Bouchier, 17th July, 1756.
5. The writings of Bynkersboek (1737), Wolff (1749) and Vattel were then given a new meaning to the laws of neutrality, and "from the somewhat incoherent practice followed by belligerents and neutrals with respect to each other during the eighteenth century, three principles disengage themselves with clearness. The neutral state was bound not to commit any act favouring one of two belligerents in matters affecting their war, and it was in turn incumbent on belligerents to respect the sovereignty of the neutral. It was also recognised, though less fully, that it is the duty of a state to restrain foreign governments and private persons from using the territory and resources of a country for belligerent purposes". Hall, International Law, p. 588.

   Cf: "I call these non-enemies who are of neither party in a war and who owe nothing by treaty to one side or to the other. If they are under any such obligation they are not mere friends but allies.................Their duty is to use all care not to meddle in the

on any account, extend assistance to one of the belligerents, in any manner whatsoever, which might influence the course of the war in favour of one against the other. It may be said that the fugitives at Fulta were no longer a flighting party. But it is also to be taken into consideration that they had not absolutely given up the idea of renewing the contest with the Nawab but had in fact appealed both to the Madras and Bombay Councils for adequate assistance to be able to reestablish their position and power upon a "secure and respectable footing"[1]. Mr. Charles Manningham had been deputed by them to the members of the Madras Council in the middle of July with a request for the supply of Military force "together with a sufficient quantity of ammunition, cannon and all other warlike stores, military and marine"[2]. Recrudescence of hostilities was only a question of better times and opportunities for them. Moreover, this conduct of the Dutch might be regarded as conforming to the practice of the age if there had been any defensive or offensive alliance between the English and the Dutch in Bengal. But the Dutch had themselves declared on a previous occassion that the treaty subsisting between the King of the Netherlands and the King of Great Britain did not apply to Bengal[3].

The English at Fulta spent their days in utmost distress and misery. But even the longest day has its end. Their adversity was over with a new turn in Bengal affairs after the arrival there of Admiral Watson and Colonel Clive. Reaching Culpee (Kalpi) on the 13th December, 1756, Admiral Watson sent the

---

war..................if I am neutral, I can not advantage one party, lest I injure the other...............The enemies of our friends may be looked at in two lights, either as our friends, or as the enemies of our friends. If they are regarded as our friends we are right in helping them with our counsel, our resources our arms and every thing which is of avail in war. But in so far as they are the enemies of our friends, we are barred from such conduct because by it we should give a preference to one party over the other, inconsistent with that equality in friendship which is above all things to be studied. It is more essential to remain in amity with both than to favour the hostilities of one at the cost of a tacit renunciation of the friendship of the other". Bynkershoek: Hall, International Law, p. 578.

1. Letter to Court from Fulta, 17th September, 1756.
2. Hill, op. cit., Vol. II, p 71; Orme, Vol. II, p. 88; Stewart, History of Bengal, p. 382.
3. Vide ante.

following note of warning to the Dutch Director, Mr. Bisdom, on the next day: "With views and designs so every way just and equitable, I fully persuade myself, I have no opposition to apprehend either secret or open from a European nation whatsoever, more especially from one, so long and so closely connected with us in the strictest alliance and friendship. Convinced of this truth, I should have deemed it unnecessary to have acquainted you with my resolution of making war on the Nawab and his subjects, had I not been made acquainted since my arrival here that he has demanded your assistance both of ship and men, to act against the subjects of the King my master, my duty to whom obliges me to acquaint you that should you grant him the assistance he demands I shall regard any such act an open declaration of war and act accordingly"[1]. The Admiral also demanded of the Dutch Director as many of their (the Dutch) pilots and masters. "capable of taking charge of ship," as could "possibly be spared"[2].

Referring to the Admiral's warning against extending assistance to the Nawab, the Dutch Director observed in reply on the 19th December, that he knew his "duty too well to enter into a course of action contrary thereto" even if that exposed him to the Nawab's 'fury'[3]. In another letter written on the 21st December, he pointed out his inability to comply with the Admiral's demand for pilots, as five of their seven pilots were ill, the navigation down to the sea was "so encumbered" that neither men nor vessels could pass, and twenty four of their vessels (with packs, bales, anchors, ropes and provisions) had been "under embargo" at Calcutta, Tanna Makwa and Buz Buz so that these may be utilised against the Nawab[4]. He also expressed therein that the Dutch having "a sincere regard for the British nation" were "mortified at their disaster", but were not in a position to be able to render them any assistance, as that would expose them to the "wrath of the Nawab"[5].

---

1. Hill, op. cit., Vol. II, pp. 54-55.
2. Ibid, pp. 56-57.
3. Ibid, p. 72.
4. Ibid.
5. Ibid.

Immediately afer the recovery of Calcutta by the English, the Dutch Director not only hastened to congratulate Admiral Watson, on the 2nd January, 1757, with "all cordiality and respect"[1], but also requested him to allow the Dutch "equipment-master"[2] Captain Lucas Zuydland, who had carried the letter of congratulation, to bring some of the Dutch vessels with provisions for their Company' ships and "to accord furthermore, a free passage up and down" for all Dutch ships[3].

But this did not serve to promote perfect cordiality between the Dutch and the English. While the English were marching against Hugli, a sloop of one of their ships, lying between Calcutta and Baranagore, removed by force one of the Dutch "quarter-masters" from a Dutch brigantine, lying before Baranagore, and engaged him as pilot in the said ship. The Dutch Director strongly protested against it on the 8th January, 1757, and demanded release of the "said pressed sailor", so that the Nawab might not accuse the Dutch of having lent that man to the English with the object of helping the fulfilment of their designs[4].

The Dutch at Hugli must have been subject to great inconveniences during its siege by the English. To avoid the evil effects of warfare as far as possible and because of what the Dutch described as "acts of insolence" on the part of the victorious soldiery, may peaceful inhabitants of Chinsura and Hugli deserted those places. The Dutch Director requested Captain Smith and Major Kilpatrick to "issue strict orders" for the cessation[5] of such acts but to no effect. The Nawab's march from Murshidabad with a large force also caused considerable anxiety in their minds, as they were not certain how he would behave towards them[6]. In such a "critical juncture of affairs", they resolved to send all their women to their factory near Cassimbazar to be sojourned there till the danger was over[7]. Further,

1. Ibid, p. 78.
2. In the opinion of Mr. S.C. Hill, he corresponds to "a master attendant, the officer in general charge of the shipping".
3. Hill, op. cit., Vol. II, p. 78.
4. Ibid.
5. Ibid, p. 101.
6. Ibid, p. 102.
7. Ibid.

the prevailing confusion made it difficult for them to be fully vigilant about the movements of the people at Hugli and the ingress or egress of goods into or from that city.

To add to the gravity of the situation, not only did Admiral Watson ignore the Dutch Director's request and remonstrance, but higly indignant at his noncompliance with all his demands, he accused the Dutch on the 11th January of having acted against English interests by sheltering some subjects of the Nawab with their effects and by permitting the use of their guns against the English at Hugli[1]. He demanded of Mr. Bisdom the "immediate delivery of every subject of the Nawab's (who had taken shelter with him) with their effects" to Captain Smith of His Britannic Majesty's ship the Bridgwater[2]. Taken aback at the Admiral's imperious attitude, the Dutch Director pleaded innocence of his people in the matter, and sent to him the following reply on the 12th January: "It appears to me from your Excellency's missive of yesterday, as if the expression of feelings of grattitude for the services rendered by us to the British nation in the days of distress is to consist only of words and that our fair dealings and uprightness are in danger of being rewarded with the devastation of our colony and an attack upon our fort, as your Excellency attached credit to accusations not one word of which is true and as to-day, already, a lieutenant with a small armed force has commenced to use force within the precincts of our town to pillage the houses of our old inhabitants, in direct opposition to the tenor of the Manifesto sent us by Governor Drake and the Council at Calcutta. We have granted protection to no one save to our own inhabitants, and in regard to the charge concerning the removal of our cannon, it is inconceivable how your Excellency can accept such false reports. Why not rather make enquiries into the matter among the English sojourning here, if a true report about us is what is wanted, but if our ruin is what is aimed at we must leave our cause in the hands of God, and, in the measure of our weakness, meet force with force, I myself entertaining no doubt but that I shall, by virtue of my inno-

1. Ibid.
2. Ibid.

cence, be able to justify my action both here and in Europe"[1].

Admiral Watson sent Captain Henry Speke to Mr. Bisdom to discuss matters with him. Captain Speke also charged the Dutch with a gross violation of neutrality. He urged on the 15th January that the Dutch Government had not observed the prohibition regarding the purchase by their people of "merchandise or any part of the pillage made upon the English at the capture of Calcutta" and that when the English wanted to recover their merchandise, stocked in a private house at Chinsura, it passed out of that place at their connivance before the very eyes of the latter[2]. He further complained that on the day after the capture of Hugli, the Dutch sheltered at Chinsura some "Moors of the highest rank". Mr. Bisdom was asked to afford the English all facilities in their searches for the goods and persons of the Nawab's people[3].

Mr. Bisdom wrote a strong letter of protest to Admiral Watson on the 16th January against what he considered to be "acts of violence and insolent conduct"[4]. In another, dated the 18th Jaunary, he held that the Dutch could not be charged with violation of neutrality and of the "published prohibition", as, during the siege of Hugli, most of their servants had fled away, which made it impossible for them to prevent others from coming in or going out of their place and making any purchases there. As regards the allegation that he had given shelter to some "Moors of consideration", he replied that he had none with him save one Jubbo, half-brother of Wajid, an inhabitant of that village, a nephew of Mirza Reza, who was accustomed to sojourn every year at Chinsura on his return from Dacca, and a Persian who had been living there since the time of Director Huyghens. Further, he refused to comply with his demand for the inventory of the goods of those inhabitants, on whose houses he (i. e., Mr. Bisdom) had placed guards, because, in his opinion, that would give offence to the Nawab and would be at the same time prejudicial to "the legal privileges of the

1. Ibid, pp. 99-100.
2. Ibid, pp. 106-108.
3. Ibid.
4. Ibid, pp. 108-110.

indwellers"[1]. Two Dutch Captains, and many Dutch vessels, while sailing downwards were detained by the English. The Dutch Council complained on the 18th January that this was not only an insult to their 'flag' but was also responsible for causing them "great inconvenience and loss in despatching ships". They sent two of their members, Armenault and Bacheracht, on deputation to the Council in Calcutta to enquire into the reasons of such a procedure, whereupon a "license was granted for the release of one and all"[2].

On the 22nd January, the Dutch Council expressed their feelings of gratitude on the favourable results of their deputation and even intimated to Admiral Watson that they were ready to mediate between the English and the Nawab for amicable settlement of their disputes[3]. But this proposal did not materialise, though a new turn in the situation compelled the Nawab to conclude the treaty of the 9th February, 1757. Their intercession, at the request of the Frenchmen at Chandernagore to prevent British attack on that place, also proved fruitless[4].

The Dutch found themselves placed in a delicate situation during the British siege and capture of the French settlement of Chandernagore (14th-23rd March). Their active participation in the affairs connected with this incident was out of the question because of their weak position, of which they were fully conscious. "...... our Fort is a nest", observed the Dutch Council at Hugli in its letter to the Assembly of Seventeen, dated 2nd April, 1757, "that would not be able to withstand the onslaught of enemy for as many hours as the French have days, and now the English have destroyed the imaginary neutrality within the Ganges, the stronger party will, in the future, no doubt always assail and ruin the weaker unless the parties at variance can find a means to reconcile their clashing interests". But owing to the proximity of their settlement to Chandernagore, they naturally apprehended prejudial influence of what was happening there on themselves. To obviate that they wisely considered obser-

1. Ibid, pp. 111-112.
2. Ibid, pp. 88-82 and pp. 112-113.
3. Ibid, p. 128.
4. Ibid, p. 247.

vance of perfect neutrality to be the safest course for them, and tried to satisfy the Nawab as well as the English[1]. Many French fugitives from the besieged city of Chandernagore took shelter at Chinsura and Hugli with their women and children. But on Colonel Clive's demand for their delivery on the 13th April[2], Adrian Bisdom asked them to quit Dutch territory. The fugitives, according to Colonel Clive's order, repaired first to Calcutta and subsequently to Chandernagore and Serampur[3]. In conformity with the principle of neutrality, Mr. Vernet, Chief of the Dutch Factory near Cassimbazar, did not comply with the request of the Chief of the English factory at Cassimbazar for a small barrel of powder and also paid no heed to the "urgent solicitations" of the Seths, the famous bankers of Murshidabad, for "the storage of some goods of the French that they had taken in pawn for debt"[4]. The Dutch Council at Chinsura whole-heartedly approved of this course of action on the part of Mr. Vernet. They even thought of some precautionary steps for the future to obviate the adverse effects of a renewed contest between the English and the French. Thus they solicited the permission of their authorities at Batavia to get their settlement strongly fortified and prayed them for supply of 24 pounders or at least 18 as they had "seen during the siege of Fort Oreans (at Chandernagore), the great use of heavy guns on the bastions for destroying the batteries of the besiegers"[5].

But what the Dutch apprehended was not to happen. French influence in Bengal had been shattered irretrievably in March, 1757, and its quick decline in other parts of India came almost as an inevitable corollary to the mighty political revolution that took place in Bengal in the course of a few months. Siraj-ud-daulah's star had already began to pale and Plassey sealed his doom. The English, who were the principal actors in the drama that was then staged on the political chess-board of Bengal, indeed found themselvs elevated to an immenesely improved

---

1. Ibid, pp. 289-291.
2. Ibid, p. 326.
3. Ibid, p. 347.
4. Ibid, p. 320.
5. Ibid, p. 348.

position[1]. On the 10th June, the Dutch Director, Mr. Bisdom, congratulated Colonel Clive, the hero of the hour, in the following words : "As you have had the principal charge of the enterprise against the late Nawab Suraj-u-Dawlah, we can not refrain from congratulating you upon your success. Wishing that the arms of His Brittanic Majesty may everywhere prosper and be triumphant, and that your fame, Sir, may become more renowned, we have the honour to be, with much consideration, etc., etc."[2]

---

1. Clive's Letter William Pitt the Elder, dated 7th January, 1759.
2. Malcolm, Life of Clive, Vol II, p. 70, foot-note.

CHAPTER III

BEDARA

Circumstances leading to Bedara

Bisdom's congratulation of Clive on his victory at Plassey was but a formal affair. In reality the Dutch grew extremely jealous of consequent English ascendancy in Bengal and even challenged it in the course of two years and a half. They at first hesitated to recognise Mir Jafar as the Nawab of Bengal[1] and some of them at Chinsura did not even salute him, while he had been passing through that place on his way to Calcutta[2]. Mir Jafar thereupon imposed some restrictions on their trade, which were not removed till they apologised for their conduct.

Some accounts state that about the month of November, 1758, Miran, the Nawab's son, and a few officers of the Nawab's *darbar*, made him sensible of his dependent position, and created an anti-English feeling in his mind[3]. It is said that the Dutch sought to take advantage of this opportunity of "stepping forward and putting in a claim to some sort of power and influence in the province"[4]. Holwell goes so far as to write that they negotiated secretly with Mir Jafar for "transporting troops from Batavia into these provinces that with their united force a stop might be put to the power of the English. This scheme was conducted by Raja Rajballabh on the one side and Foocratoojar (Khawjah Wajid) for the Dutch on the other, about October or November 1758, the period when the Deccan expedition took place and the garrison was much reduced"[5].

---

1. Clive's letter to the Dutch Director, 2nd October, 1758. Malcolm, op. cit., Vol. II, pp. 71-72.
2. 'Lord Clive's Righthandman', p. 120.
3. Ibid, p. 122.
4. Broome, Bengal Army, p. 261.
5. Copy of the Memorial delivered by the President (Mr. Holwell) to the Select Committee upon the arrival of Mr. Vansittart to succeed him in the Government, Original Papers etc., Vol. I, pp. 8-13; 'Clive's Narrative', Malcolm, Vol. II, pp. 74-80. Grose, Voyage to the East Indies, Vol. II, p. 365. Clive's "Narrative of the Disputes with the Dutch in

But it would not be quite accurate to assert, only on such evidence, that Mir Jafar was actually implicated in such intrigues.

There could not be, however, any doubt about the Dutch menace to the English in Bengal at that time. In July, 1759[1] there was a rumour in Calcutta that the Dutch Government at Batavia had been fitting out a strong armament, which was destined for Bengal. Early in August, the arrival of a Dutch vessel in the Ganges, carrying on board a number of European and Malaya troops, gave some support to the rumour[2]. The Nawab was at first much perplexed on hearing this news from Colonel Clive, but, after a while, at his request he sent a *parawana* to the Dutch Government at Hugli strictly ordering them not to engage in hostilities or to shelter any additional troops, but to help his own troops as well as those of the English. He also asked Omarbeg Khan, *faujdar* of Hugli, to join and help the English, and demanded assistance from the latter in preventing any foreign troops or ships from coming up the river. The Dutch Government at Chinsura replied that they would implicitly obey his orders, that the vessel in the river had been driven by stress of weather from Nagapatam, which was its destination, and that it would go away as soon as it had been provided with water and provisions. But this did not satisfy Clive. He posted troops at Tannah's Fort and Charnock's Battery, on either side of the river Hugli, to stop and search all vessels passing upwards and on the roads sides also to prevent the advance of any troops by land[3]. When the Dutch at

---

Bengal"has been inserted in Malcolm's 'Life of Clive', Vol. II. Malcolm notes that "This paper is not dated but from a correction in the rough copy of it (it) appears to have been drawn up in November, 1759; and was, no doubt, transmitted to England at that period".

1. Forrest, The Life of Lord Clive, Vol. II, p. 146.

2. Clive's Narrative, Malcolm, Vol. II, p. 75; Grose, Voyage to the East Indies, Vol. II, p. 365; Extracts from the Journals of Archibald Swinton printed in Bengal: Past and Present, January-March, 1926, pp. 3-38; Broome, Bengal Army, p. 262.

3. Clive's Narrative, Malcolm, Vol. II, p. 75; Grose, op. cit., Vol. II, p. 366. Mynheer Lucas Zuydland, the Dutch Master-Attendant, "refused to allow his boat to be searched when passing up, and struck the officer on duty at Charnock's Battery for which he was put into guard, and on searching his Budgerow, 18 Malaya soldiers were found concealed on board; these were sent back to their ship, and Mynheer Zuydland was then released; formal remonstrances were now received from the Dutch

Chinsura remonstrated, the Council in Calcutta replied, "....as principals, we had, by the custom and laws of nations, a right to search all vessels whatever advancing up this river, not knowing but they might introduce French troops into the country; and that as auxiliaries to the Moghal, we were under a necessity, by solemn treaty, to join his Viceroy in opposing the inroduction of any European or foreign troops whatever into Bengal; and that we should absolutely and religiously do our duty to the utmost of our strength and power in both capacities." The Dutch vessel soon sailed away.

But again, early in the month of October, six or seven Dutch vessels, full of European as well as Malaya troops, arrived at the mouth of the river Hugli. Mir Jafar, who had then come to Calcutta on a visit to Colonel Clive, was at first greatly disconcerted on receiving this news[1]. But soon he expressed his intention to proceed to Hugli in order to compel the Dutch to send away their vessels and troops, or else to drive them out of the province for ever. So leaving Calcutta on the 19th October, he reached Khawjah Wajid's garden, half way between Hugli and Chinsura, where he met the Dutch agents and held some consultations with them. After three or four days, he wrote to Colonel Clive that he had granted "some indulgence" to the Dutch in their trade, and they "had engaged to leave the river with their ships and troops as soon the season would permit."

Holwell asserts that the Dutch troops arrived at the invitation of the Nawab, who was implicated in a secret conspiracy with them. "The (Dutch) armament", he writes, "arrived during his visit; his stay after that was short, his mind much embarrassed, and his whole subsequent conduct gave most undoubted proofs, that the Dutch forces were arrived, by his invitation. That such were the sentiments of Colonel Clive and the Council, appears from the narrative of that Dutch business transmitted to the Honourable Court of Directors and to our several admirals; a perusal of this narrative will convince the impartial

---

to which equally formal replies and arguments were returned. At length the vessel departed and matters returned to their usual state of quiet."

1. Clive's Narrative, Malcolm, op. cit., Vol. II, p. 76.

that the Nabob, in his behaviour on this occasion, was guilty of alliance and that from this period no terms whatever should have been preserved with him after such unexampled treachery and ingratitude....that the Nabob's real intentions never were to distress effectually that people but on the contrary, were only aimed to amuse and deceive us......"[1]. Warren Hastings thought that the Nawab's real intention was not to chastise but to favour the Dutch. He wrote to Clive : "Every day's transactions confirm me more and more in the opinion that the Nabob is acting a treacherous part with you"[2]. Broome also accuses Mir Jafar of double-dealing in this matter[3]. Among the modern writers, Malleson entertains no doubt about "secret understanding between the Dutch and the Nawab"[4]. Sir George Forrest emphatically writes : "He had invited the Dutch, but on hearing of their arrival he assumed an oriental air of indifference which western diplomats cannot imitate with success"[5]. But the Council in Calcutta observed in its letter to the Court of Directors, dated, the 22nd October, 1759 : "We think it necessary to inform you the Dutch are attempting to disturb the tranquillity of this province by introducing into this country a considerable body of Europeans and Buggoses (Malaya soldiers) unknown to the Subah (Nawab), this illjudged step has greatly exasperated him against them and we have reason to believe that matters will shortly be accommodated by those Forces being obliged to leave the River". It is clear from this note that the Council in Calcutta, expected to be most intimately acquainted with the state of affairs in Bengal, did not consider the Nawab guilty of forming any anti-English conspiracy with thc Dutch. It was not then certainly possible for him to expel the Dutch from Bengal, and so he tried to accommodate matters by a policy of conciliation. Most probably, this not being in agreement with what Holwell and Hastings desired for severe chastisment of the Dutch, was construed by them as a treacherous move on the

1. Holwell's Memorial, Original Papers, Vol. I, pp. 8-13; Holwell, Indian Tracts, p. 11.
2. Quoted in Forrest, The Life of Lord Clive, Vol. ii, p. 153.
3. Broome, op. cit., p. 263.
4. Malleson, The Decisive Battles of India, p. 122.
5. Forrest, The Life of Lord Clive, Vol. II, p. 153.

part of the Nawab.

Commencement of Hostilities

Determined to strike a blow against the English the Dutch were moving up the river with their vessels and engaged themselves in enlisting sepoys at Chinsura, Cassimbazar and Patna[1]. The Dutch vessels carried 700 European infantry and 800 Malaya soldiers which could act in combination with the Dutch garrison at Chinsura consisting of about 150 Europeans including artillery and a large number of sepoys. The English force consisted of 250 European infantry, a company of about 80 strong artillery with *lascars* attached and about 1,200 sepoys. A party of European infantry and 500 sepoys of the English were at Patna; a part of the battalion and a number of sepoys were stationed at Midnapore to oppose the incursion of the Marathas, and some detachments of sepoys were stationed at Chittagong, Dacca, Murshidabad and Burdwan. All military men, scattered in different parts of the country, were ordered to come back to Calcutta, and the militia of Calcutta, composed of the European, Armenian and Portuguese inhabitants under the command of Mr. Holwell, were charged with the defence of the Fort and the town. "The only vessels in the river were three Indiamen, the 'Duke of Dorset' of 544 tons, Captain Forrester; 'the Calcutta' of 761 tons Captain Wilson; and 'the Hardwicke' of 573 tons Captain Sampson, with 'the Leopard, Snow' and a small ship under Captain Barclay. The latter vessel was immediately set off with an express to Admiral Cornish, then cruising on the Arracan coast, requesting immediate assistance"[2].

Colonel Clive ordered three Indiamen, 'The Calcutta', 'The Duke of Dorset', and 'the Hardwicke' to proceed to the defence of the town, and the detachments at Tannah's fort (five miles below Calcutta on the right bank of the Hugli river) and Char-

1. Clive's Narrative, Malcolm, Vol. II, pp. 76-79; Grose, op. cit, Vol. II, p. 368.
2. Clive's Narrative, Malcolm, Vol. II, pp. 82-84 : Broome, Bengal Army, p. 265.

nock's Battery (nearly opposite to Tannah's fort) were strengthened[1]. The command of the parties at those two places was entrusted to Captain Knox. Colonel Forde, who had at the time returned from Masulipatam to Bengal, took up the command of the entire body of troops in the garrison[2]. He wrote to the Nawab[3] in strong and peremptory terms to send his son with an army to invest Chinsura, but was not listened to.

The Dutch now remonstrated against the actions of the English in searching their boats and obstructing the advance of their troops up the river, and threatened them with immediate and full revenge if they persisted in doing so. But the English replied that "they (the English) had given no insult to their (Dutch) colours, or attacked or touched their property or infringed their privileges; that with respect to their bringing troops into Bengal, the Nabob knew best how far it was incumbent on him to preserve the peace and tranquillity of his country; that their boats had been stopped and searched, and the advance of their troops opposed, by orders from the Viceroy, and under the Emperor his master's colours, and by his troops; that they must apply therefore to him"[4].

This greatly enraged the Dutch, who commenced hostilities by capturing seven English vessels including the 'Leopard Snow' and the 'Captain Barclay', tearing down English colours, disembarking their guns, military stores, etc., from their ships, and making prisoners of their Captains and crews. At Fulta and Raipore they tore down English flags and burnt the houses and effects of the English Company's tenants. Clive informed the Nawab that these acts of violence on the part of the Dutch meant nothing short of their commencing "actual war against English", that "he would leave chastising the Dutch" to the English and "desist from sending either his son or any part of his army to their assistance", but that, if he desired to convince the English of his sincerity, "he should directly surround their subordinates,

1. Clive's Narrative, Malcolm, Vol. II, 80; Grose, op. cit., Vol. II, p. 368.
2. Clive's Narrative, Malcolm, Vol. II, p. 84.
3. Ibid, p. 80.
4. Ibid; Grose, op. cit., Vol. II, p. 369.
5. Ibid; Clive's Narrative, Malcolm, Vol. II, p. 82.

and distress them in the country to the utmost"[1]. The Dutch, on their part, described the English as the aggressors and solicited Mir Jafar's favour. Thus Bisdom, the Dutch Director at Chinsura, wrote to the Nawab: "The troops were not called here at my own desire, nor did I imagine they would have ever come to action, and fully intended to have returned them by the ships when they sailed for Europe; they were brought here for the security of the ships. This I acquainted your Excellency of several times. During their stay in camp they molested no man, nor had any disturbances with the country people; this also you are well assured of. It was never my intention they should fight; but the English hoisted Moor's colours, and immediately came down upon them and a battle ensued. Your Excellency is the magistrate of justice and therefore I desire you will interfere. I was desirous some advantage should arise to the ryots from the sale of the goods when they were brought up, and intended to have laden on board the ships the saltpetre and other goods that were brought, and with the people that came here, despatched them to Europe; but the English would not permit the boats to pass. I am willing to act up to your agreement and hope Your Excellency will adhere to it also. In this we entirely depend on your favour. The Company have for a long time carried on trade here, and therefore earnestly desire you will continue to them your favour and protection as we are not able of ourselves to root out our enemies" [2].

Clive lost no time to take adequate steps to oppose the Dutch. In view of the gravity of the situation he took upon himself the responsibility of ordering of hostile acts against a nation with whom his own country was then at peace in Europe. He subsequently told the Select Committee of the House of Commons that "he was sensible how very critical his situation was at that time; that he risked his life and fortune in taking up himself to commence hostilities against a nation, with whom we were at peace; but that he knew the fate of Bengal and of the Company depended upon it."

According to Clive's instructions, Forde started from Calcutta

---

1. Ibid, p. 83.
2. Quoted in Forrest, The Life o. Lord Clive, Vol. II, p. 156.

on the 16th November with a strong detachment to capture the Dutch factory at Baranagore. Mr. Bisdom and his Council thereupon wrote to Clive on the 18th November: "We have received, with the utmost surprise, the disagreeable news, that some of your European dependants, accompanied by one hundred and fifty sepoys, came this morning to Baranagore, and demanded the keys of our Company's house there, and afterwards hoisted thereon the English flag. Now as we neither can nor must construe such an act any otherwise than as an open aggression and hostility, and an actual declaration of war; so we have just grounds, and find ourselves under the highest necessity, to demand the reasons of such hostilities, as far exceed all the bounds of equity and justice; and at the same time, in the name of our honour, to complain and protest on that head; and moreover, to demand again reparation and satisfaction for such crying acts of violence, and to insist on sufficient security and assurance or at least, in case of refusal, a positive and categorical answer. In which last case, we require that we may be informed immediately whether you are resolved to declare war against us; or, without previous declaration, commence it; and, besides, in consequence of this, that you acquaint us as soon as possible, whether the aforesaid troops were authorised by you to so hostile a conduct; and whether or no they are to proceed further by your order"[1]. This was followed next day by the following letter: "Last night, on sending off our letter to you, gentlemen, we had the fresh mortification, not without the greatest surprise, to see ourselves insulted in the hostile manner by your dependents, supported by some sepoys, as, in coming down the river, they had the assurance, within sight and reach of our forts, to fire sharp shot on our vessels lying here at anchor. We cannot help thinking, and with reason, but that these reiterated acts of violence have been committed by your orders; a fresh indication that you appear plainly no longer to make any account of the most solemn treaties, subsisting between your crown and our state since you thus venture, to break through them. We could not, however, omit acquainting you therewith by these presents, and we doubt not you will readily and natu-

1. Grose, op. cit., Vol. II, p. 371.

rally judge that it can not be taken amiss of us, or in the least misconstrued, if we now inform you, that we have been constrained to recede, in this case, from our wanted moderation, and with force to repel such disturbers of the peace; having found by experience there was no dealing with such persons without employing the like compulsory means. You therefore must and can lay the blame of the consequences arising from such dangerous proceedings, on no body but yourselves. We therefore further exhort you, gentlemen, not to suffer yourselves to be betrayed into any pernicious resolution, through the false and illgrounded reports of these sepoys, who may have brought you any account of this affair; but rather consider this our conduct as an effect of the justice of that self-defence which we have been compelled to use. On the other hand, you may be assured, that we are far from acting offensively in any respect against any one, much less against you; but that in every step we take, we seek and aim at nothing else, as we have already mentioned in our former letter, than under the blessing of heaven, to defend ourselves against all hostile attacks and acts of violence whatever; and to do nothing in our present circumstances, but what may stand justified in the sight both of God and man; and what the interests of the settlements, rights and privileges, entrusted to our care, by our lords and masters, may require at our hands"[1].

On the 20th November, Colonel Forde seized the Dutch factory at Baranagore and "passed over the river with the troops and four field artillery of Serampore, the Danish factory, and marched towards Chandernagore; not only with a view of striking terror into Chinsura, but to be ready to intercept the Dutch troops in case they should disembark, and attempt to gain that place by land"[2]. On the 21st November, the Dutch armament came to anchor in Sankeral Reach, just out of cannon shot from the English batteries. On the 22nd or 23rd November, the Dutch landed on the western bank seven hundred Europeans and about eight hundred Malaya soldiers. On the same day Colonel Clive sent orders to Commodore Wilson to demand of

1. Ibid, pp, 372-73.
2. Malcolm, op. cit., Vol. II, p. 84.

the Dutch immediate restitution of their ships, subjects and property or "to fight, sink, burn and destroy the Dutch ships on their refusal". On the 24th, the demand was made but was not complied with. The English, thereupon, attacked the Dutch, notwithstanding the inferiority of their own vessels (the Dutch having seven ships)[1]. After two hours' fighting, the Dutch Commodore struck, and all the other vessels followed the example; except his second, who fought his way swiftly as far low as Culpee, where, however, he was very soon captured by the 'Oxford' and the 'Royal George', which had arrived two days ago with orders to join the other Captains. On this occasion, the Dutch lost more than 100 men; on board the Dutch Commodore's ship, the Vlissingen, upwards of 30 men were killed and double that number wounded. On the side of the English, 'the Duke of Dorset' suffered considerably[2].

On the same day, Colonel Forde, while marching through Chandernagore, was attacked by a Dutch garrison, which had gone from Chinsura the previous evening with 720 Europeans and 300 sepoys and had taken up a position amidst the ruined buildings of Chandernagore with four pieces of cannon. But he drove them from that position, captured their cannon and chased them furiously up to Chinsura[3]. In the evening, he was joined by Captain Knox and the troops from the Charnock's and Tannah batteries. He soon received intelligence that the Dutch troops from the ships, joined by a part of the garrison from Chinsura, were advancing, and so immediately resolved to attack them on the plains of Bedara, about 4 miles from Chinsura[4]. He wrote to Clive for explicit official orders regarding his course of action. Clive was then engaged in playing cards, and without leaving the table, he wrote an answer on the

1. List of the Dutch fleet: – The Vlissingen, Bleiswyk, Welgeleegen, and the Princes of Orange of 36 guns each, the Elizabeth Dorothea and Waereld of 26 guns each, and de Mossel of 16 guns. Grose, op. cit., Vol. II, p. 374, footnote.
2. Clive's Narrative, Malcolm, Vol. II, pp. 85-86; Grose, op. cit., Vol. II, pp. 374-75.
3. Ibid.
4. Malcolm, op. cit., Vol. II, p. 86.
   Grose. op. cit., Vol. II, p. 375.

back of the letter in pencil, "Dear Forde, Fight them immediately, I will send you the Order of Council tomorrow"[1]. On receipt of this permission early in the morning of the 25th, he marched at once with two field-pieces and met the Dutch on the plains of Bedara (midway between Chandernagore and Chinsura). Thus ensued on the soil of Bengal a deadly contest between two rival European powers, which has been described by Clive himself in the following manner: "The Dutch were commanded by Colonel Roussel, a French soldier of fortune. They consisted of nearly seven hundred Europeans, and as many buggoses, besides country troops; ours of two hundred and forty infantry and eighty of the train, and fifty more Europeans composing the troops of horses, independents and volunteers, and about eight hundred sepoys. The engagement was short, bloody, and decisive. The Dutch were put to a total rout in less than half an hour; they had about one hundred and twenty Europeans, and two hundred buggoses killed, three hundred and fifty Europeans and about one hudred and fifty wounded. Our loss was inconsiderable"[2]. After this action, Colonel Forde returned, sat down before Chinsura and wrote for further orders. "The Dutch were now as abject in their submission as they had been insolent in their supposed superiority"[3]. They wrote to Colonel

1. Malcolm, op. cit., Vol. II. p. 87. Colonel Lionel Forde has quoted the following version of this incident from Hough's 'Military Events in India', Vol. I, p. 20, footnote: "When Colonel Forde reported to Clive the arrival of the Dutch in the river and wrote for orders, Clive was playing at cards and wrote on the back of the nine of diamonds: 'Fight them and I will send you an order in Council tomorrow"; Lord Clive's Righthandman, p. 186.

2. Vide Appendix 'S, (1...11...111) in 'Lord Clive's Righthandman'.

3. Clive's Narrative, Malcolm, op. cit., Vol. II. p. 87; Proceedings, 28th November, 1759, A. D. Compare with this the Dutch account of the battle of Bedara :—"On the 25th, when the troops and other hands, which, on the 22nd before, were gone on shore, in their projected march, came Chandernagore, they were there met by the 'English' who according to their own account, to the number of 1170, were posted very advantageously, and provided with a numerous artillery. No sooner were these troops come within cannon shot, but they were fired on by the English : and though all the people were extremely fatigued by a very long march, which they were obliged to make for the space of three days; yet with much bravery, they stood the fire of the English; and, though unprovided of any artillery marched up with a full and steady pace to the enemy; but meeting in their way a broad and deep ditch, which they were constrained to pass, to avoid being destroyed by the artillery of the English, the troops in passing that ditch, fell

Forde and also to the Council in Calcutta soliciting cessation of hostilities and with proposals for amity[1].

Effects of Bedara

The English readily responded to the request of the vanquished Dutch. "Deputies were appointed and things brought to a speedy and amicable conclusion"[2]. On the 3rd December, 1759, the Dutch "disavowed the proceedings of their ships below, acknowledged themselves the aggressors, and agreed to pay costs and damages", whilst the English agreed that "these terms being fulfilled, they would restore the ships, stores and prisoners they had captured, except those of the latter, who desired to enter their service"[3].

But three days after the battle of Bedara, the Dutch had to face a new danger. Miran marched from Murshidabad with six or seven thousand horse and encamped within two miles of Chinsura avowedly to exterminate the Dutch as they had disturbed peace in Bengal. Highly terrified at this, the Dutch implored British protection. Clive now "displayed", as Malleson notes, "a mastery of statesmanship, the greater as it bore the

---

into some disorder : the English, taking advantage of these circumstances, redoubled the fire of their artillery and musquetry : and the disorder, already risen, being thereby increased, caused the slaughter of a part of these troops; another part was made prisoners; and the rest were constrained to retire". Grose, op. cit., Vol. II, p. 376, footnote.

1. Clive's Narrative, Malcolm, op. cit., Vol. II, p. 86.
2. About this time Mr. John Burdett, Chief of the English factory at Balasore, "had put peons on the Dutch Factory and had secured the persons of two Dutch-men residing there". The Council in Calcutta on receipt of this news from Mr. Burdett's letter of 1st December, 1759, replied to him in the following manner :—.........We are much surprised at the manner of his proceeding against the Dutch, and that we direct he, immediately on the receipt of our letter, releases the Dutch gentlemen and takes off the peons from their factory; and further, he apologises to them for his conduct on this occasion, and acquaints them that what he had done is from a misunderstanding of our orders and is totally disapproved by us". Proceedings, 8 December, 1759 A. D.
3. Clive's Narrative, Malcolm, op. cit., Vol. II, p. 88.

appearance of signal generosity"[1]. By timely intervention on behalf of the Dutch he effected an accommodation between them and Miran. It was ratified on the 5th December, 1759. Miran forgave the Dutch and promised protection to their trade and privileges on the following terms :—that they shall never meditate war, introduce or enlist troops, or raise fortifications in the country; that they shall be allowed to keep up one hundred and twenty-five European soldiers, and no more, for the service of their factories of Chinsura, Cassimbazar, and Patna; that they shall forthwith send their ships and remaining troops out of country; and that violation of any one of these articles will subject them to utter expulsion[2].

Thus the "attempts of the Dutch to rival the political power of the English in Bengal" ended in smoke. Bedara "decisively foiled", remarks Malleson significantly, "the attempt to establish an Indo-Batavian empire"[3]. Politically it dealt a crushing blow to Dutch ambition, and the position of the Dutch became dependent on the goodwill of their erstwhile enemy, the English East India Company. Further, their commerce which had been previously "very profitable, now ceased to be so"[4]. The Dutch traveller, Stavorinus, who visited Bengal during 1769-71 A. D., writes : "Since the unfortunate issue of our expedition to Bengal in 1759, the reputation of our countrymen has been on the decline; and we are obliged to be not a little dependent upon the English, with respect to the piece-goods wanted for our cargoes, both for Batavia and for Holland". As for the English, the defeat and humiliation of the Dutch relieved them of a great menace. "Thus ended an affair", observed Clive, "which, had the event been different, threatened us in its consequences with utter destruction........". Bedara also supplemented Plassey and considerably added to British influence in Bengal. Broome exultingly remarks : "Such was the brilliant victory of Bedarrah marked by an extraordinary degree of skill and courage, and most important in its results"[5].

---

1. Malleson, op. cit., p. 123.
2. Clive's Narrative, Malcolm, op. cit., Vol. II, p. 86.
3. Malleson, op. cit., p. 124.
4. Stavorinus, Voyage to the East Indies, Vol. I, pp. 499-501.
5. Broome, Bengal Army, p. 270.

CHAPTER IV

Post Bedara Period, 1759-72

Strained Relations after Bedara

The convention of the 3rd December, 1759, between the Dutch and the English in Bengal, and that of the 5th December, 1759, between the Dutch and Miran, could not promote cordial relations among these powers, as their interests were still highly conflicting. A contemporary Dutch account [1] charaterised these "as two extorted conventions", and there is no doubt that they reduced the Dutch in Bengal to a position of absolute dependence on the English and the Nawab for all practical purposes. The Dutch must have consequently nursed in their hearts feelings of discontent and resentment, which goaded them to make attempts for recovery of what they had lost by exploitation of opportunities in the course of occasional political disturbances within the province. They tried to avail themselves of one such opportunity when the Nawab of Bengal and the English East India Company were faced with a critical situation between 1759 and 1761. The Zamindars like Kamgar Khan Main of Narhat in the Gaya District, the Rajas of Birbhum, Burdwan and Vishnupur (in the Bankura District) and a few others, and Khadim Husain Khan, Governor of Purnea, were then hostile to the Nawab's Government, portions of western Bengal were subject to ravages of the Marathas under Sheo Bhat Sathe [2] who "gave out that he came to support the cause of the Emperor"[3], Shah Alam II encouraged by some local disaffected Zamindars [4] invaded Bihar and Bengal, the "English force in Bengal was

---

1. A fresh complaint lately exhibited to the States of Holland and West Friezland by the Dutch East India Company against the servants of the English East India Company in Bengal, 2nd December, 1761.
2. Long, Selections, Nos. 537, 539, 558;
   C. P. C., Vol. I, p. 40 and p. 46.
3. Broome, op. cit., p. 289.
4. Sarkar, F. M. E., II, pp. 534-43;
   C. P. C., Vol. I, p. 46.

much divided, and Moorshedabad, the population of which was inclined to disaffection, as was also a portion of the troops stationed there, was left entirely defenceless" [1]. The Dutch in Bengal and Bihar then actually tried to co-operate with some of the malcontents [2] and the Prince invader.

Mir Jafar accused the Dutch of being engaged in "a private correspondence" with his "known and public enemies" [3], and of having "tendered and promised their assistance to the Mogul Prince (Ali Gohur), who was in full march against" him [4]. Two significant letters [5] show that the charge was not groundless. In one Rajah Ramnarain, *naib nazim* of Bihar, wrote to the Dutch : "Your Bravery and capacity has (have) been represented by my friend Meer Seid Allee Cawn Bahadur to His Majesty (Shah Alam II) after the conclusion of the affairs of the Sircar. Whatsoever you shall represent to the King shall be granted by the means of Seid Mahmud Afzul Cawn because the said Seid attends on his Majesty and is my entire friend". In another, Shah Alam II addressed the Dutch as follows : "Your loyal attachment and faithful services and duty and obedience have been set forth in the Royal presence both by our trusty servant Meer Said Alle Cawn Bahadur in person and by the addresses of the Noble Seid Mahomed Afzul Cawn wherefore we have dispatched the said noble Seid from our Court to you. It behoves you what so ever commands he shall deliver to you from us to look upon it as authentic and act accordingly thereto. Be in every respect satisfied and attend with Diligence and zeal to the care of the Royal Country. By the will of God you will become shortly worthy object of the Royal Favour and protection. This caution is given you for your conduct".

The assurances of Shah Alam II, who himself was then being driven from pillar to post and post to pillar, proved to be abortive. Emperor in name he was then, in fact, a helpless wanderer,

1. Broome, op. cit., p. 288.
2. C. P. C., Vol. I, p. 30.
   Long, op. cit., p. 235.
3. Public Proceedings, 12th May, 1760.
4. A Fresh Complaint, etc,
5. Quoted in Public consultations, 5th August, 1761.

a "broken adventurer"[1], subject to vicissitudes of fortune and like a drowning man trying to catch at a straw. Major Carnac aptly observed in his letter to the Select Committee in Calcutta, written on the 6th March, 1761, about three years after he had escorted Shah Alam from Gaya to Patna, that "the unhappy Prince is reduced so low, as to be much more an object of pity than of fear"[2].

On the other hand, the attempted alliance between Shah Alam II and the Dutch subjected the latter to reprisals from Mir Jafar. On the 11th February, 1760, the Nawab sent a large army under the command of Kasim Khan against the Dutch at Hugli. The Dutch Company's fort Gustavas was invested by them in such a way as to make it impossible for their servants to get provisions of any kind[3]. Kasim Khan soon ordered for razing all the outworks of the Fort and demanded of the Dutch a considerable sum of money as penalty or fine. The Dutch argued that the charge against them was a false one, and so the Commander's demand was totally unjust. But it was of no avail. They were compelled "to raze the outworks of the Fort, and to buy off further Acts of violence by paying him 50,000 Florins"[4].

Again, in the month of April of the same year, the Nawab accused the Dutch of levying men, and sent for the Chief of their Factory at Cassimbazar[5] for an explanation. The said Chief could not turn up owing to his illness. But De-Wilde, the Second of that Factory, went before the Nawab, who "on admitting him into his presence, repeated the above-mentioned accusation, adding that the Company's servants held a correspondence and conspired with his Enemies"[6]. He "demanded of the (Dutch) Company, by way of contribution, an immense sum of fifty laks of rupees, or two and twenty Tons and a half of Gold; threatening if this sum was not immediately paid, to level with the ground the Company's settlements"[7]. De

---

1. Broome, op. cit., p. 278.
2. Vansittarts's Narrative, Vol. I, p. 185.
3. A Fresh Complaint, etc.
4. Ibid.
5. Ibid.
6. Ibid.
7. Ibid.

Wilde tried his utmost to prove the falsity of these accusations and argued that the sepoys in the Dutch Company's service had been maintained to guard the effects of the Company against the apprehended inroads of the Marathas, and that the natives in their service would have been already discharged but for that unexpected investment of their factory. But all his arguments mingled with the air. The Nawab put him under arrest, caused the Dutch factory at Cassimbazar to be invested by his troops, and posted 11 pieces of cannon before it. The Dutch warded off the immediate destruction of their factory by the payment of seven and a half tons of gold, and by promising to discharge the sepoys and send back the remainder of the troops to Hugli. This promise they fulfilled very soon; but their factory still remained invested by the Nawab's troops. When the Dutch insisted on their withdrawal, the Nawab replied that "it was not in the Prince's Breast but in that of the English"[1], though, in fact, the Nawab himself was determined to punish the Dutch. He wrote to Mr. Holwell, the acting Governor of Calcutta :

"Notwithstanding the solemn treaties and engagements in which we have lately entered with the Dutch and which we on our parts have faithfully adhered to and kept, they without any just cause and contrary to their faith and word have broke, by carrying on a private correspondence with our known and public enemies, by keeping up a much larger force, than we thought proper to allow them by the late treaty, and which they themselves agreed to and also by repairing the works ordered to be pulled down at their factory of Chinsura, in which place they are now employed in making quantities of powder and many other military preparations, which but too plainly show the wickedness of their designs and intention, against my honour, the peace and safety of my kingdom. Being therefore now come to a resolution of punishing the said offenders who have so long abused my clemency and goodness I propose sending down a large force to their factory at Chinsura to oblige them by force, since other means will not do, to keep to their promises and oaths, and to agree to the just conditions I shall impose on them to prevent in time their plots and wicked designs, and to secure

1. Ibid.

the quiet of my country from their evil attempts,"[1].

But nothing was then possible without the consent of the English. So the Dutch sought their intervention to secure withdrawal of the Nawab's troops. Mr. Holwell wrote a letter to Mr. Bisdom on the 15th May, 1760, wherein "under the semblance of friendship" he advised the Dutch to satisfy the demands of the Nawab. He expressed his desire to mediate between the Dutch and the Nawab so that the English might be relieved, as he noted, of the necessity of playing a 'very disagreeable part'.

Convention of August, 1760

Accordingly, two commissioners were sent by the Dutch to Calcutta on the 29th May. After about two months and a half, they entered, under guarantee of the President and Council at Fort William, into a more precise convention with the Nawab, on the 23rd August, 1760[2]. The articles of the convention were very hard for the Dutch, especially the sixth one. It laid down : "The Director and Council of the Dutch Company shall now and at all times, whenever, the Nabob may require it, permit one of his officers, accompanied by one of the English, to muster or visit their troops and Military Stores at Chinsura and their other factories; or if any other means can be agreed on between the Governor and Council of Fort William and the Director and Council of Chinsura, whereby the Governor and Council of Fort William may, to their satisfaction, be assured of the Number of their troops and the quantity of their military stores, and he, as umpire, empowered to give a satisfactory Answer to the Nabob, as to the security of his country; that then, and in that case the Nabob would no further insist on the Muster". According to the other articles, the Dutch were required :—(1) to send away from Chinsura and other factories all the troops exceeding the number of 125 men, (II) not to raise any new works of fortifications, and to demolish those which they had erected since the last treaty with the Nawab, (III) to

1. Proceedings, 12th May, 1760.
2. Foreign Consultations, 25th August, 1760. Vide Appendix E.

send away from their factories the surplus number of artillery, and the quantity of warlike stores, (IV) not to suffer "above one European ship at once to come up higher than Culpi, Foltha (Fulta), or Mayapur, without, previously obtaining of the Nawab an Express permission". Umid Ray, the Nawab's Diwan, also promised that as soon as the Dutch had submitted to those conditions, their trade in Bengal, Bihar and Orissa "shall be carried on free and unmolested in all points whatever, except the saltpetre Trade", which would remain exclusively in the hands of the English; that they "shall not be aggrieved with any new or unusual Extortions of Money, under what pretence so ever", and that "in future their business in the Mint shall continue to be carried on, without the least molestation or obstruction".

The convention of August, 1760, undoubtedly reduced the Dutch in Bengal to a humilating and precarious position. Many of them leaving their ships at Fulta and Chinsura, proceeded towards Birbhum, the Rajah of which place was then not on friendly terms with the Nawab[1]. But the Nawab at once sent a company of troops to intercept them at Dewanganj in Burdwan and to bring them over to Calcutta. The local authorities in the interior of Burdwan and the inhabitants of Dewanganj were also warned not to allow the Dutch to enter into the territory of the Raja of Birbhum. The Dutch not only found their prestige damaged but their material interests through trade were also severely affected.

Appeal of the Dutch to their Home Authorities

In these circumstances, the Directors of the General Dutch East India Company appealed to the Government of the Netherlands that they might recommend to their ministers at the Court of England, "to insist in the strongest manner, on a proper satisfaction for the injuries sustained, as also on the actual Reparation of the Damage and detriment undergone; and at the same time write to the said ministers, above all to insist with his Britannic Majesty, that in the meantime, necessary orders may,

1. Long, p. 235.

on the first proper opportunity, be expedited to the Ind es; in which both the commanders of His Majesty's squadrons there, and the servants of the English Company in Bengal, and elsewhere in the Indies, where it may be necessary shall be expressly forbid, in virtue of the Treaty or convention, entered in the year 1757, with the then Nabob of Bengal, as Allies of the Nabob, or under any other Pretext or Violence against the Dutch Company, their settlements or dependents, and in which they, on the contrary, shall be charged to behave in regard to the Company of this country, according to the Tenor of the Treaties subsisting between his Britannic Majesty and their High Mightinesses; and, moreover, to suffer the commerce of the said Company to be carried on unmolested, and without giving them the least Impediment or Let therein"[1]. The Dutch Directors pointed out in their pettition that the servants of the English East India Company in Bengal were helping the Nawab against them on the strength of the treaty of 1757[2] and prayed that it might be cancelled, as in their opinion it directly clashed with the treaties, concluded between the King of the Netherlands and the King of Great Britain.

Technically speaking, according to Article XIII of the said treaty, the English pledged themselves to help Mir Jafar against his enemies, and it is also true that, for sometime, there was no love lost between the Nawab and the Dutch. Of course, under the plea of helping the Nawab the English had, on many occassions, adopted hostile measures against the Dutch in order to 'feed fat their ancient grudge' on their old commercial rival in Bengal, for which the Dutch might justly complain. But their demand for cancellation of the treaty between Mir Jafar and the English, on the ground that it clashed with treaties existing between the two powers in Europe, does not seem to have been a just one. We have already seen that when the English had, during the invasion of Calcutta by Siraj-ud-daulah, sought the help of the Dutch on the basis of these treaties, the latter had themselves plainly declared that their treaties in Europe did not apply to their colonies in India[3]. To ask then for can-

1. A Fresh Complaint, etc.
2. Stewart, History of Bengal, Appendix No. XIII.
3. Vide ante.

cellation of that treaty was to hope against hope. Moreover, judging from the point of view of practical politics, it may be said that the English could not do away with that treaty which had been so greatly instrumental in enhancing their influence.

To remove these complaints of the Directors of the Dutch East India Company, the States General of Netherlands began preparations for sending an armament to India. Fortunately, the Right Hon'ble the Earl of Bute, Secretary of State, was able to diagnose the real state of affairs. He signified to the Court of Directors that there was reason to "apprehend the Dutch East India Company extremely anxious at the situation of their affairs in Bengal may induce the States General to take such measures as may produce the most fatal consequence and become perhaps the cause of a rupture between the two powers in those parts, if the utmost care and precaution be not used without delay to prevent it...."[1], and recommended to them, in the most serious manner, to try their level best to remove the unhappy disputes subsisting between the two nations. The Court of Directors in England, therefore, sent the following orders to the Council in Calcutta "....You do not commit any hostility or act of violence against the Dutch Company's agents; on the contrary, you are to use your best endeavours to cultivate by all sorts of good offices a reciprocal friendship and good understanding with them, and in particular if the Nawab shall unjustly attempt to molest the Dutch Company in Bengal, or any way prejudice them in their trade, privileges or property, you are to interpose your good offices in order to procure them redress and satisfaction; and if these should prove ineffectual, you are to aid and defend them to the utmost of your power, it being our sincere desire and intention that the Dutch Company shall enjoy freedom of trade, safety and protection equally with ourselves"[2].

Relation of the Dutch with the English and the Nawab still uncordial

In spite of this, perfect harmony between the two was out of

---

1. Court's Letter, April 2, 1762, para. 19.
2. Ibid.

the question. In 1763 the English Company's Resident at Maldah complained to the Council in Calcutta that the *gomastas* of the Dutch had been greatly obstructing the English investments there by their clandestine purchases from the weavers engaged by the English Company[1]. But there were no violent frictions. The English in Calcutta received the news of what has been described as the Patna massacre of 1763 in a correspondence from the Dutch at Chinsura who had come to know of it through a letter written by John Bacheracht, Chief of the Dutch factory at Patna, and Mr. Andries Surgon Schultz, Second of that factory, to Louis Taillefert and others of the Council at Chinsura on the 27th June, 1763[2]. In the same year, the disputes between the English and the Dutch factories at Patna concerning the opium trade there were also amicably settled. Referring to this, the Court of Directors observed in their letter to the Calcutta Council, dated the 22nd February, 1764. "We are extremely glad to find from your letter of the 14th February, 1763, that the disagreeable altercations and disputes between the English and the Dutch Factories concerning the Opium Trade have been accommodated by the President, when he was at Patna, to the satisfaction of both parties. As there is reason to believe that both our servants, and those of the Dutch, have been to blame, we strictly charge it upon you to see that the conduct of our servants in providing or purchasing this article is such as may prevent every reason for complaint, and on the other hand the greatest care must be taken that the Dutch behave in like manner to ours. Willing as we are that every occasion for disputes, with the Dutch should be industriously avoided, and that harmony and friendship should be cultivated with the greatest care between the two Companies and their respective servants in India, yet a due attention must be always paid to prevent their infringing or breaking in upon our just rights and privileges, and a strict eye must be kept upon all their motions.....". On repetition of complaints by the Dutch regarding obstructions to their trade in saltpetre and opium at Patna, similar instructions were communicated by the Court of

1. Proceedings, 23rd June, 1763.
2. Proceedings, 11th July, 1763.

Directors to the Council in Calcutta in their letter, dated the 15th February, 1765.

Results of the Battle of Buxar in October, 1764, and grant of *Diwani* by the Delhi Emperor, Shah Alam II, to the English in August, 1765, made the English the real masters of the Bengal Subah. To reap full benefit out of their new position they wanted to avoid then any serious disputes with the European Companies, with whose countries they were in peace. "We are very glad", wrote the Court of Directors to the Council in Calcutta on the 24th December, 1765, "you have had no disputes of a public nature with the Dutch. As all foreign nations will be Jealous of our growing power, you should take great care not to encroach on their rights and give them just cause of offence. At the same time the like attention must be paid to the just rights and privileges of the Company in any of your transactions with their representatives, observing however, all the moderation that is due to the friendship at present subsisting between our respective sovereigns".

The Court again wrote on the 17th May, 1766. "We may reasonably expect the other European nations would be jealous of our growing power in Bengal. It must, therefore, be a particular object of our attention to give them no just cause of complaint but to let them possess the same privileges they are entitled to. Great care should be taken that our servants in the 'subordinates' (subordinate factories), and our *Gomastahs* at the *Aurungs* do not impede them in their investments."

But the Dutch still felt that the comparative weakness of their position had exposed them to certain disadvantages, and with the usual psychology of a disappointed party they continued to murmur against these. There were occasionally some frivolous disputes, which the Court of Directors considered to be "mere indications of their envy at the growth of a power they cannot check". In 1767, the Dutch at Chinsura complained to Mr. Verelst, the English Governor in Calcutta, that their boats were very often detained at the customs-houses by the *Chaukidars*[1]. The *Chaukidars* could not be fully blamed for this, as they were perfectly entitled to discharge their functions of en‹uiring

1. C. P. C., Vol. II, p. 47.

into the nature of the goods carried on vessels of the European Companies and of realising duties from them. But at the same time it was necessary to manage things in such a way as should serve to remove the causes of complaint on the part of the Dutch and others. After having duly considered the matter, Mr. Verelst asked Muhammad Reza Khan, the *naib nazim* at Murshidabad, to take necessary steps to redress the grievances of the Dutch. He was instructed to see that the *dastaks* attached to the boats of the European Companies contained all necessary details regarding the goods they carried and that the boats were searched at all the recognised customs-stations. The Governor observed : "If no search is made at Serampur, Jellingy (Jalangi) and Rajmahal, the *sarkar* will be defrauded of its revenues, as the said European people will be free to trade in all the *mahals* lying between these *chowkies* without paying any duties. Also they will be able to land and sell their goods duty-free at any place on this side of Azimabad as far as the *chauki* of Rajmahal. The result will be that all the trade of that part of the country will fall into their hands. When the English and other merchants do not object to their goods and boats being searched there does not seem to be any reason why the Dutch and the French should"[1].

Muhammad Reza Khan assured the Governor on the 21st March, 1767, that whenever the Dutch *vakil* "represents a grievance of this nature to him," he "never omits to give a severe reprimand to the *chaukidars* and to insist on their abstaining from illegal practices"[2]. Thus when the Dutch complained early in 1767 that the *chaukidar* of Bhutmari had unjustly detained their boats and had exacted more than the usual duties the latter was "ordered to refund the money which he had misappropriated and was dismissed from his post"[3].

But the growing control of the English over the opium business in Bihar proved to be a cause of friction between the Dutch and the English. The English East India Company had established a monopoly of opium manufacture and trade in Bihar in 1761[4]. Henceforth they permitted the other Euro-

1. Copies of Persian Letters issued, 1766-67, No. 4.
2. C. P. C., II, pp. 52-53.
3. Ibid.
4. Monckton Jones, Warren Hastings in Bengal, p. 231.

pean companies to purchase only a limited quantity of this article[1]. The Dutch murmured against this practice and addressed in protest several memorials to Mr. Verelst[2]. Mr. Verelst ordered Muhammad Reza Khan on the 12th March, 1767, to remove such obstacles as prevented the Dutch from enjoying their due share in the opium business[3]. This was in conformity with the instructions of the Court of Directors, communicated in their letter to the Council in Calcutta, dated the 17th May, 1766 : "........do not obstruct the Dutch in their opium trade which is an object of such importance to them that any difficulties they may be laid under in this part of their investment will certainly be attended with very disagreeable altercations between the two Companies in Europe, and must, as much as possible, be avoided." The Governor was in favour of the opium business "being left free to all people so that the revenues of the *sarkar* may suffer no diminution"[4]. Muhammad Reza Khan promised to obey his 'commands'[5] implicitly and directed Raja Shitab Ray, *naib nazim* of Bihar, "to put the opium trade on the footing of the original regulation, giving free license to all on payment of the duties and strictly prohibiting its being engrossed by one individual, to give the Dutch likewise on their satisfying the *paikars*, liberty to purchase........"[6]. Mr. Verelst did not fail to consider the risks of this "open door" policy in opium trade. So, while disposed to allow the Dutch to "make fair and equitable purchase from the *paikars*"[7], he wanted that they should not "aim at grasping the whole business"[8]. He informed Muhammad Reza Khan that if they attempted to do so they must be "deprived of their share in the business altogether, and the 'open door' closed to them"[9].

Another important cause of misunderstanding between the

---

1. Valentia's Travels, Vol. I, pp. 68-69.
2. C. P. C., Vol. II, p. 47.
3. Ibid.
4. Ibid.
5. Ibid, p. 52.
6. Ibid.
7. Ibid, p. 47.
8. Ibid.
9. Ibid.

English and the Dutch during this period was the "uncommon scarcity of weavers"[1] throughout Bengal. As this was producing adverse effects on the investment of all the European trading Companies[2], *gomastas* of each one of them tried "to seduce the weavers"[3] from the service of the other. Already during the Governorship of Lord Clive, the *gomastas* of the respective Companies complained against one another on the charge of 'monopolising' the weavers[4]. Lord Clive and Verelst, then a member of the Council, tried[5] to bring about a settlement of this dispute. The Dutch proposed a "distribution of the *tantis* (weavers)"[6] among the European Companies. The Governor assented to this proposal "on the condition that the complaints of the Dutch should be first enquired into"[7], and a 'joint Commission' was appointed for this purpose[8].

The Commission could not effect any solution of the problem during Clive's administration. Well alive to the evil consequences of this situation, Mr. Verelst pointed out to the Court of Directors, in his letter of the 17th March, 1767, the necessity of coming "to some equitable compromise with the other European establishments"[9] on this matter. But before the Commissioners could resume their work, the Dutch demanded that "the enumeration of the *tantis* should take place first"[10], though the English insisted on preliminary enquiries being made into their complaints[11]. The Dutch Council at Chinsura wrote to the English on the 14th June, 1767 : "In Bengal the workmen by your servants are obliged against their will, and thanks to take money and to bind themselves not to work for anybody else but for the English. This, gentlemen, is a fact, which we take

---

1. Letter from Verelst to the Court of Directors, dated the 17th March, 1767.
2. Ibid.
3. Ibid.
4. C. P. C., II, p. 122; Bolts, Considerations, etc., p. 73 and p. 192.
5. C. P. C., II, p. 122.
6. Ibid.
7. Ibid.
8. Ibid.
9. Verelst, View, etc., p. 99.
10. C. P. C., II, p. 122.
11. Ibid.

for granted, that the greatest part among you cannot say that you are ignorant of"[1].

Mr. Verelst was of opinion that the 'partition' of the weavers would not only "be a difficult and lengthy business"[2], but would also "bring the Nizamat into contempt"[3]. He, therefore, considered it advisable to consult the Nawab and his officers on this matter, and referred it to them. Strongly objecting to it they replied to the following effect: "This would be impossible, besides it will cause great distress to the *tantis*. If a distribution of them takes place, they will have to accept the price they are offered and will not be able to sell their goods to the highest bidder. The merchants of this country will be deprived of their just privileges and ultimately of the necessities of life. The output of the goods will diminish to such an extent that it will not suffice even for the people of this country. And what is more important, there will be a considerable fall in the revenues of the *Sarkar*"[4].

Mr. Verelst regarded the views of the Nizamat officials to be just and did not acqiesce in the demands of the Dutch for the 'partition' of weavers. The Dutch were, however, granted some new concessions as a result of which, it was hoped, "the output of the goods will increase"[5]. At the request of the English Governor, the Nawab's Government "promised to encourage the *tantis* by reducing the *abwabs* and other taxes"[6] and "to refrain from demanding the *mangan* (a cess levied to pay the allowances of the officers at customs-houses and landing places) from the Dutch merchants and obstructing them without a just cause"[7].

But the relations between the Dutch and the Nawab's Government did not even now turn out to be very cordial. The Dutch had annexed the village of Partabpur near Hugli to their territory, and Mirza Kazim, formerly *naib* of the *faujdar* of

1. Long, No. 947.
2. C. P. C., II, p. 122.
3. Ibid.
4. Ibid.
5. Ibid.
6. Ibid.
7. Ibid.

Hugli and an inhabitant of that village, had connived at this encroachment on their part out of some personal considerations. Muhammad Reza Khan visited Hugli in February, 1768, argued before the Dutch Director, Mr. G. L. Vernet, that Partabpur was within the area of Hugli and was "never annexed to Chinsura", and asked him to restore it to the Nawab[1]. Certain other objectionable acts on the part of the Dutch excited displeasure of the Nawab's Government against them. The duties due from the Dutch Company for conveying goods up and down the river Ganges had not been paid by Mr. Vernet to the Nawab's government for several years. The Nawab thereupon ordered the *faujdar* of Hugli to exact his lawful dues in a forcible manner, and the latter accordingly sent a *chubdar* to the Dutch Governor demanding the money and threatening him that "in case it were not paid, he would not suffer any more goods belonging to the Dutch to pass"[2]. The Director "took umbrage at this peremptory message, and after having violently abused the poor *chaubdar* sent him to the fiscal De Saumaise, and had him bound to the whipping post, and unmercifully flogged"[3]. At this the *faujdar* of Hugli detained all callicoes and other piece-goods intended as cargoes for the Dutch ships, which were to sail for Europe in the month of November 1768, and he also invested Chinsura on the landside on 3rd October, 1768, with ten or twelve soldiers[4]. All the "approaches and barriers were so closely guarded that no one could go in or out. This occasioned in the ensuing days such a scarcity of provisions, among the inhabitants of the village, that many of them perished for want. ....Besides this blockade in the land side, the Moors (the Muslims) had also beset the river, above the village, so that nothing would be brought down the water; and from below, while there was little to be obtained, while there was any rice, seven pounds weight were sold for a rupee, but it was soon consumed"[5]. This state of things being referred by Mr. Vernet to the Dutch Council, the latter in consideration of the futility

1. Ibid, pp. 231-32.
2. Stavorinus, op. cit., Vol. I, p. 115.
3. Ibid.
4. Ibid.
5. Ibid.

of force decided to settle the matter amicably through the mediation of the English. A Dutch deputation consisting of Mr. Ross, the Chief Administrator, and Mr. Vam Braam, the Controller of Equipments, settled the affair with the English Council in Calcutta and Muhammad Reza Khan. The Nawab's government being assured that the arrear duties would be quickly paid, the Dutch goods were released, the Nawab's soldiers left Chinsura on the 15th October, and navigation of the river was opened[1].

But both the English and the Nawab's Government still kept a strict watch on the movements of the Dutch. They were required by the *Naib Nazim* "not to send more than one European with a fleet"[2]. Officers were appointed at Kalpi to inspect their ships as also of the other Europeans like the French and the Danes to take account of the cannon, arms and military stores on board their ships and to prevent them from sailing up the Kalpi with more than 24 guns and stores in proportion and 250 men in one ship which were considered sufficient for a merchant vessel[3]. These officers were ordered "not to use violence without just cause........and on no account to receive gratuities from any"[4]. But the regulations of the Nizamat were not duly obeyed by the Dutch, the French and even the Danes[5]. Rather, they impeded the work of the *faujdari* and occasionally oppressed the people[6]. Mr. John Cartier, successor of Mr. Verelst as the Governor in Calcutta, asked Muhammad Reza Khan to write to the *faujdari* at Hugli to take necessary steps against such illegal actions on the part of the Dutch[7]. But nothing effective seems to have been done.

---

1. Ibid.
2. Calendar of Persian Correspondence, Vol. III, p. 27.
3. Ibid, p. 42.
4. Ibid.
5. Ibid, p. 138.
6. Ibid, pp. 249-50.
7. Ibid, p. 255.

CHAPTER V

Warren Hastings and The Dutch

Demand on the Dutch for Copies of their Firmans

The relations between the Dutch at Chinsura and the Nawab's government at Murshidabad continued to be strained during the administration of John Cartier, and there were occasional disputes between them. Probably with a view to preventing their repetitions, Warren Hastings wrote to Nawab Mubarak-ud-daulah on the 11th May, 1773, to ask the Dutch Director to produce copies of those *firmans* on the strength of which his Company claimed various privileges in Bengal[1]. The Nawab acted accordingly, before the close of that month, through Khan Jahan Khan, the newly appointed *faujdar* of Hugli[2]. But the Dutch Director defied the authority of Khan Jahan Khan, who thereupon requested Hastings to "give him definite directions for his guidance" and to persuade the Nawab at Murshidabad to authorise him to stop Dutch trading vessels[3]. As desired by Hastings, the Nawab issued a *parwanah* to the *faujdar* of Hugli asking him therein to assert his authority duly[4].

General Economic Decline and the European Companies

Warren Hastings' government was concerned with the Dutch in several other ways during that period of transition. The mid-eighteenth century political revolutions in Bengal naturally produced highly pernicious effects on the economic condition of the province, and the country was in no time doomed to a pathetic economic decline, complete recovery from which has still remained an unrealised dream in spite of the gigantic strides of modernism. The various economic abuses having originated in

---

1. Ibid, Vol. IV, p. 56.
2. Ibid, p. 64.
3. Ibid, p. 149.
4. Ibid, pp. 161-62.

the pre-Plassey period[1] found scope for development after 1757 owing to the collapse of sound governance, prevalence of widesprerad disorder throughout the country, and rapacity of the East India Company's employees. In consequence of the enhanced influence of the English East India Company after the battle of Plassey, "many innovations", writes Vansittart, "were practised by some of the Company's servants, or the people employed under their authority"[2]. Orme significantly observes : "....as it is the nature of man to err with great changes of fortune, many, not content with the undisputed advantages accruing from the revolution, immediately began to trade in salt and other articles, which had hitherto been prohibited to all Europeans; and Mir Jafar complained of those encroachments within a month after his accession; which, although checked for the present, were afterwards renewed, and at last produced much more mischief than even disinterested sagacity could have foreseen"[3]. Mir Qasim complained justly that "a trade was carried on in all sorts of goods, such as it was never yet the custom to trade in".[4] We are told by Harry Verelst, a contemporary Bengal officer of the English East India Company, that "a trade was carried on without payment of duties in the prosecution of which infinite oppressions were committed. English agents and Gomastahs, not contented with injuring the people, trampled on the authority of the Government, binding and punishing the Nabob's officers wherever they presumed to interfere"[5].

With misrule, disorder, corruption, and oppression rampant throughout the length and breadth of Bengal, Bihar and Orissa, the miseries of the local people, as we know from copious references in the accounts of contemporary writers and records of the English and other European trading companies, knew no bounds. Referring to the condition of Bengal in 1765, the Select Committee in Bengal observed in their letter to the Court of Directors, dated the 19th February, 1767:—"We beheld a presi-

1. K. K. Datta, Bengal Subah, Vol. I, pp. 438-39.
2. Vansittart's Narrative, Vol. I, p. 24.
3. Orme's Indostan, Vol. II, p. 189,
4. Original Papers Relating to the Disturbances in Bengal from 1759-63, Vol. I, pp. 170-73.
5. Verelst, View of Bengal, p. 48.

dency divided, headstrong and licentious, a Government without nerves, a treasury without money, and service without subordination, discipline or public spirit......amidst a general stagnation of useful industry and of licensed commerce, individuals were accumulating riches, which they had ravished from the insulted prince and his helpless people who groaned under the united pressure of discontent, poverty and oppression". Richard Becher, an experienced servant of the English Company, wrote to the Secret Committee of the Court of Directors on the 24th May, 1769: "It must give pain to an Englishman to have reason to think that since the accession of the Company to the Dewani the condition of the people of this country has been worse than it was before; and yet I am afraid the fact is undoubted....this fine country which flourished under the most despotic and arbitrary government, is verging towards its Ruin".

At the same time, this state of affairs could not but cause great hardships and disadvantages to the French and the Dutch in Bengal. Not only was the political influence of both destroyed under the stress of the quickly succeeding revolutions throughout India, but their commerce too was hard hit. It is true that acts of reprisals were not absolutely wanting on their part[1]. But these only served to offend the English and the Nawab's government instead of improving their lot in any way.

As it has been previously noted, in view of the repeated complaints of the Dutch, the Court of Directors in England sometimes instructed the Council in Calcutta[2] to redress their grievances as far as possible, and occasionally agreements were actually entered into by the Dutch and the English to prevent "altercations and disputes" between them.[3] These, however, had only temporary effect, and the Dutch did not cease from complaining against what they considered to be their legitimate grievances during the administrations of Harry Verelst and John Cartier.

During the next few years the Court of Directors reiterated

---

1. There are some references regarding this point in Calendar of Persian Correspondence, Vols. II & III & IV.
2. Court's letters, dated (a) 2nd April, 1762, (b) 17th May, 1766.
3. Letter from the Council in Calcutta to the Court of Directors, dated 14th February, 1763; Stavorinus, op. cit., Vol. I, p. 115.

their orders to the Council in Calcutta to enquire into the complaints of the Dutch in Bengal regarding what they pointed out to be interruptions to their trade and the latter referred these to a Committee of Aurungs which had been constituted in 1755 with the President and three other members of the Council in Calcutta. Agreeing with the Council in Calcutta that the plea of the Dutch for receiving larger quantity of saltpetre from the English than what had been supplied to them for the last few years, "appears to be wholly invalidated and indeed seems to have been relinquished by their receiving the same proportions in other years without any objection", the Court of Directors wrote to the Council in Calcutta on the 25th March, 1772 : "We have, therefore, only to enjoin you at all times to promote that concord and good understanding which we are solicitious to preserve with the subjects of the States General by affording the Dutch as large a proportion out of the annual produce of saltpetre as can be spared from our own occasions, allowing at the same time for a reasonable share to the agents of other European nations with whom we are also desirous to be on terms of harmony and friendship".[1]

Anglo-Dutch Attempts to settle mutual Differences

The regulation of Bengal's internal trade formed an item in Warren Hastings' programme of administrative reforms, and as such he had to take notice of the complaints of the Dutch. In 1772 he issued orders for "Freedom of Trade" of the Dutch Company.[2] The Council in Calcutta wrote to the Court of Directors on the 10th November, 1772 : "With the Dutch we have had the most friendly intercourse of late and we doubt not of maintaining the same in time to come." In the month of December, 1773, Hastings passed an order by which "the former Embargo laid upon the Exportation of Grain" by the Dutch was "entirely taken off".[3]

1. Letters from the Court of Directors to the Council in Calcutta, 13th September, 1768, para 60, and 23rd March, 1770, para 49.
2. Secret Consultations, 1 May, 1775, No. I.
3. Letters from the Dutch Council at Hugli to the Governor and Council of Fort William at Calcutta, dated 18th December and 24th December 1773; Public Consultations, 3rd January, 1774, Nos. 6 & 7.

In 1772, Mr. Bacheracht, the Dutch Director at Chinsura, and Mr. Falk, Chief of the Dutch Factory at Patna, represented against their payment of an annual tribute of Rs. 30,000 to the Bihar government[1]. Mr. Hastings tried, during his short stay at Patna in 1773-74, to accomodate the differences between the Dutch and the English on this question. This tribute had been paid by the Dutch to the *naib nazim* at Patna for over fifty years and was claimed subsequently by the English Government. Its payment originated in the year 1716 when a small sum was paid to the Bihar Government in return for the protection afforded by them to Dutch trade against the harassing activities of the Chakwars.[2] As Mr. Bacheracht held that even after this protection was discontinued the amount of tribute was augmented till it rose to Rs. 30,000, out of which a sum of Rs. 15,000 was appropriated for use of the government, Rs. 10,500 were given to the Diwan and other officers, and the remainder was required for the purchase of various articles presented to them. He objected to the continuance of this tribute by pointing out that the condition for its original payment had not been long complied with, and that the officers who received a large share of it for the good offices occasionally rendered by them to the Dutch in their relation with the Nawab's government were no longer in a position either to help or to injure them after the recent political revolutious in Bengal.

But Hastings sought to establish "legality of the claim" for realisation of the tribute by the following arguments : "It is not the business of the present government to scrutinise the Records of half a century past in order to invalidate its own Rights. By whatever means, however, violent or unjust, the claim in question was first enforced, an allowed possession on one part, and an acquiescence on the other during so long a period stamps it with the sanction of a Prescriptive Right and this is consonant to the Universal Law of Nations.

By immemorial usage the established Fees paid to the Ministers of Government are the Dues of office and may be virtually

1. Vide Appendix F.
2. A powerful Hindu tribe with their stronghold at Sambho in the Begusarai Subdivision of the District of Monghyr, Vide K. K. Datta, Alivardi and His Times, p. 14.

considered as the Property of Government itself, in as much as they form a part of the Emoluments of its servants and stand in the place of actual salaries which otherwise be a charge on the public treasury.

These fees also having been paid during a length of years and in the same proportions or with little variation have obtained the same Right of Prescription"[1].

Hastings was, however, inclined to reduce the amount in such a manner that Rs. 15,000 were to be paid annually to the "Public Treasury for the use of the Government" and Rs. 5,000 to the Diwan at Patna as "as his due". The Dutch did not agree to this arrangement. Mr. Bacheracht asserted "illegality" of the tribute and repeated his representation to Hastings for its entire abolition.[2] Nothing was done immediately in this respect.

But an agreement was effected in the same year regarding the supply of saltpetre to the Dutch from Patna. This was, however, considered by the Dutch Council at Hugli to be too inadequate to satisfy their need. They wrote to the Council in Calcutta early in November, 1774: "We, therefore, beg you will take into consideration, that we have received so little (of saltpetre) for these several years past, that it does not in the least agree with the stipulated written agreement in the year, 1774, and that the Dutch Company suffer greatly by it; you will therefore be pleased to grant us the highly necessary Redress, and so far increase our share of this year's produce that it may the more agree with your's......justice".[3] The Council in Calcutta communicated to them on the 7th November, 1774 : "In Reply to the Letter you were pleased to address us on the subject of salpetre we beg leave to inform you that we are restricted from increasing the Quantity of your annual allowance by the orders of our Superiors they finding that the amount of what falls to their own share is hardly sufficient for their own Demand"[4]

Dutch Memorial to the Council In Calcutta

Towards the end of the year 1774 the Council in Calcutta

1. Secret Consultations, 10th February, 1774, No. 3.
2. Ibid, No. 4.
3. Secret Consultations, 7th November, 1774, No. 4.
4. Secret Consultations, 7th November, 1774, No. 5.

informed the Dutch at Hugli of the new system of government established at Fort William in Bengal according to the Regulating Act, and at the same time "expressed a desire of procuring a complete good understanding with respect to the interests" of their different "Establishments" by granting them all possible assistance to enable them to carry on as before their "ancient lawfully constituted trade in these countries".[1] Relying on this promise, the Dutch sent two members of their Council, Messrs. Van Dankelman and Eilbracht, on deputation to the Council in Calcutta, in the month of April, 1775. Their envoys carried a Memorial to be delivered to the Calcutta Council and were also authorised to answer every question that the English would "find proper and necessary to ask them by way of a more nice interpretation of these matters and their proposals".[2] The object of the Dutch in submitting the Memorial was thus stated by them:— "....being resolved to display to you in as brief and succint a manner as will be possible, all those disappointments and obstacles we have been forced to struggle with during the last 18 years; by which means no other prospect is left us for the future but a continual fear of some of those Mischiefs at last bursting forth into the Total ruin of our Company's Affairs in these regions if a speedy and dexterous Remedy should still remain unapplied for, We have corrected in writing a memorial concerning these matters......"[3]

In this Memorial,[4] the Dutch sought to demonstrate how their old rights and privileges based on numerous *firmans* received from Indian rulers and governors had been infringed upon from time to time; and they prayed that these might be put upon their former footing. The special points of their complaint were the vexations and obstructions from which their trade in such important articles as cotton cloths, saltpetre, opium, raw silk and silk stuffs, suffered; the opressions of the English Com-

---

1. Letter from the Dutch Council at Hugli to the Council in Calcutta, dated the 15th April, 1775; Secret Consultations, 25th April, 1775, No. 1.
2. Ibid.
3. Ibid.
4. A copy of the Memorial is embodied in Secret Consultations, 25th April, 1775, No. 2. Vide Appendix 'G'.

pany's people on them; the practice of paying *peshkash* to procure saltpetre at Patna; the embarrassments in the sphere of currency; disputes with the successive *faujdars* of Hugli on the point of jurisdiction over the inhabitants of that place; and hindrance caused to them by the stoppage of their vessels at the numerous *chowkies* (customs-stations). The Memorial in conclusion contained a proposal for the exchange of the Dutch settlement of Baranagore with some plot of land, in the circle or environs of Chinsura, equivalent to the extent of Baranagore.

The Dutch envoys were allowed to be present at the meeting of the Council in Calcutta, held on the 25th April, 1775, where they duly delivered the Memorial.[1] The Council in Calcutta sent the following reply[2] to the Dutch Council at Hugli on the 29th April, 1775 :—

"The Discussion and Investigation of the several articles contained in your Memorial will require some time as it will be necessary for us to write to our distant Factories for copies of Records and other documents respecting them. But you may depend upon our bestowing the Nicest attention and as much to as we can spare from the calls of our other urgent affairs upon this investigation, that we may bring it to a satisfactory and speedy conclusion. In the mean time we beg leave to observe that as your Memorial is only a general representation of grievances without any specification of the objects aimed at for their redress, it would be our endeavours to afford you satisfaction therein if you would be pleased to state to us your particular grievances, your pretensions formed into precise articles applied to each head of your Memorial.

"Messrs. Van Dankelman and Eilbracht having verbally and in a Letter presented to us on the 28th instant requested that we would instantly publish orders in all places where cloth manufacturers are established or other articles produced that the Trade of the Dutch Company may be carried on freely and without molestation in the same footing with our own and in the manner directed by the Mogul's Firmans etc., we have thought it proper to Cause a present publication to be issued which we conceive

1. Secret Consultations, 25th April, 1775, No. 1.
2. Secret Consultations, 1st May, 1775, No. 3.

to be sufficient to produce the end proposed by this requisition of which we have the honor to enclose you a copy and for the more effectual repression of all illegal attempts to prejudice the free Trade of this Country we shall be ready at all times to receive and redress any complaints which you or your Agents may have to prefer to us or to those acting in authority under us. We beg leave to add that in all matters with respect to the privileges of your nation we shall make it our study to afford them every possible support."

When the Dutch envoys sought to obtain recognition of the validity of their old *firmans* and *sanads* by the Council in Calcutta, the latter demanded copies of them for their perusal before expressing any definite opinion in this matter[1]. Desirous of "ascertaining as minutely as possible the rights and privileges here before enjoyed by the Dutch Company in the commerce" of saltpetre and opium in Bihar, the Council in Calcutta wrote to Isaac Sage, Chief of the English Council at Patna, on the 12th June, 1775, to consult the records of the government from "the earliest period of the establishment" of the Dutch factory at Patna and to transmit to them "particular information on those heads". He was also asked to communicate to the Council whatever he could know, as exactly as possible, regarding the "state and origin" of the tribute paid by the Dutch to the Bihar Government.[2]

A Proposed Anglo-Dutch Treaty, 1780-81

The English in India were reduced to a very critical situation in 1780, particularly owing to the successful exploits of Hyder Ali in the Carnatic who in the month of July of that year "swept down upon the plains like an avalanche carrying destruction with him" and inflicted a severe defeat on a British detachment under Colonel Baillie on the 10th September following. The news of Baillie's disaster reached the Council in Calcutta on the 23rd September, and the Governor-General himself declared in his Minute, dated the 25th September: "The calamity which has be-

1. Secret Consultations, 1st May, 1775, No. 2.
2. Secret Consultations, 12th June, 1776, No. 10.

fallen us upon the Coast, and the alarming superiority which Haider Ali Khan has acquired in the Carnatic, the despondency of the Government of Fort St. George, the consternation and distrust which seem to have spread themselves among all those who are subject to its authority, its utter want of present means and resources, the diminution of their military strength, and its declared insufficiency for the war which it is to sustain, and above all the authentic information which we have received of a great naval and military armament prepared by the Court of France and destined beyond all doubt to co-operate with Haider Ali, demand the most instant, powerful, and even hazardous exertions of the government to avert the event portended by so many concurrent difficulties." On the same day he carried a vote for the prompt despatch of reinforcements in men and money to help the semiparalysed Madras government in the prosecution of war against their powerful adversary.

The relations between Hyder and the Dutch had been rather strained since 1776 as the Dutch at Cochin did not comply with his demand to pass through their territories into Travancore. The matter was referred by the Dutch at Cochin to the Council at Batavia, and the reply of the latter concerning the demand of Hyder reached the former in the beginning of 1777. The Dutch Governor of Cochin sent this reply to Hyder's camp along with a missive and presents. In 1778 the fort at Cochin was strengthened by the Dutch commandant with seven bastions and ditches with a view to making an attempt for the recovery of the lost territory. But the Dutch could effect nothing.[1]

Though the Dutch had, during the last few years, made repeated complaints against the various impediments to which their trade in Bengal had been subjected since 1757[2] and were also suspected by the English of being engaged in secret negotiations with the Mysore government,[3] they had not yet openly taken part in any war against the English after their defeat at

1. Monumental Remains of the Dutch East India Company in the Presidency of Madras, by Alex, Rea, pp. 28-29.
2. 'A Memorial of the Dutch to Warren Hastings and the Council in Calcutta'. Secret Consultations, 25th April, 1775, No. 2.
3. Letter from William Townsed to Wililam Hornby, President of the Select Committee, Bombay, 8th May, 1775. Vide Appendix H.

Bedara in November, 1759. When, on the outbreak of war between England and France in the month of March, 1778[1] Chandernagore was captured by Lt. Colonel Alexander Dow on the 9th and the 10th July following[2], the Dutch Director and Council at Hugli wrote to the Council in Calcutta on the 11th July :—"Yesterday afternoon we had the honour to receive your letter of the 9th instant, by which you advise us that war had been declared between the Crowns of Great Britain and France and of the taking of Chandernagore. We find ourselves obliged to return thanks for this intelligence, and to declare in consequence of your request that, although we have not yet received any orders from our superiors on this subject, we shall observe the strictest neutrality"[3].

In November, 1778[4], the Dutch proposed to the Madras government the formation of an alliance against Hyder, whose march had subjected "the territory belonging to the Dutch or adjacent to Cochin" to depredations.[5] The Madras government did not immediately agree to the Dutch proposal and decided to wait till more favourable terms were offered to them. But, in view of the extremties of the then situation in the South, the Governor-General proposed, in the course of a few months, a treaty of alliance among the English, the Dutch and the Nawab of the Carnatic. The Dutch Director at Hugli, J. M. Ross, having concurred in Hastings' proposal[6] the latter sent James Lucy Dighton[7] to the Nawab of the Carantic requesting him to negotiate the proposed treaty with the Dutch at Colombo[8]. According to its terms, the Dutch were required to

---

1. Proceedings, Secret Department, Fort William, 13th July, 1778.
2. Ibid, 11th July, 1778.
3. Ibid, 14th July, 1778. The Danes at Serampore also promised to observe neutrality. Ibid, 14th July, 1778.
4. Das Gupta, The Central Authority in British India, 1774-85, pp. 141-64.
5. Calendar of Persian Correspondence, Vol. V, pp. 51-52.
6. Calendar of Persian Correspondence, Vol. VI, pp. 1-2.
7. James Lucy Dighton was soon appointed Resident on the part of the Supreme Government with the President and Select Committee of Bombay "for the purpose of transmitting such information as shall be furnished to him by that Presidency of the political state and events which have a relation to it". Proceedings, Secret Department, Fort William, 6th July, 1781.
8. Proceedings, Secret Department, Fort William, 27th April, 1781.

lend the English a body of troops of whom 1000 should be European infantry and 200 European artillerymen.[1] The former were to receive in return "not only the pay of the troops while employed, but the cession, in perpetuity, of the province of Tinnevelly, together with permission to make conquests in the neighbourhood of Cochin, and an exclusive right to the pearl fishery along the whole coast south from Ramiseram (Ramesvaram)".[2]

The negotiations for the treaty did not, however, produce the desired result, chiefly for two reasons. In the first place, the Madras government, out of certain considerations, opposed the arrangement and the Nawab of the Carnatic did not accede to its terms.[3] The latter suggested on the 11th March, 1781, that "in view of the King of England's proclamation last April, declaring the Dutch to be a neutral power, it is advisable that they should be precluded from gaining any great influence in the Carnatic"[4]. Sir Eyre Coote, who had been sent to the south of India by the Calcutta government to "stand forth and vindicate in his own person the rights and honour of the British arms" and had been previously in favour of an alliance with the Dutch[5], now shared the opinion of the Madras Council. He wrote to the Council in Calcutta on the 1st March 1781 :—"I have been informed by the Select Committee of Madras, Fort St. George, that a gentleman by name Mr. Dighton had arrived with credentials from your Board, from the Governor-General to the Nabob Walawjah for negotiating a treaty with the Dutch at Colombo or Ceylon. And where of the object appears to have been the acquisition of a military force, which, as Commander-in-chief, I certainly ought to have been consulted on, or at least had the compliment paid me of a communication distinct from the summary one which has reached in common with, and through the means of the Madras Government. But however necessary or proper this was, I have been excluded from a knowledge of every essential part of

1. Gleig, Memoris of Warren Hastings, Vol. II, p. 336 and p. 357.
2. Ibid, Vol. II, p. 337.
   Calender of Persian Correspondence, Vol. VI, p. 40.
3. Das Gupta, op. cit., p. 145.
4. Calendar of Persian Correspondence, Vol. VI, p. 40.
5. Das Gupta, op. cit., pp. 141-142.

the business either as to its origin or the grounds and principles upon which it has been resolved to prosecute it. This gentleman is so gross and unmerited a neglect and when contrasted with the conduct of your government towards Brigadier-General Goddard (whose pretensions to a superior confidence cannot be brought in comparison); when it was resolved to make peace with the Maharattas, and I may add on every occasion, that I cannot help experiencing as an indignity to both my person and station, and I must gratify the impulse of my feeling by adding, that it is an ill return to those personal fatigues and anxieties which I now undergo in the cause of the Hon'ble East India Company and the nation, and which I had every reason, from the solemn assurances, pledged to me by each member of Government, to hope, would as far as rested with them, rather have been lessened than increased. I will only add injustice to myself on this subject, as far as particulars have been come to my knowledge, that I disapprove of the negotiation proposed with the Dutch as both impolitic and unconsitutional".[1]

Secondly, the Dutch themselves procrastinated.[2] Before the treaty could be actually drawn up and ratified, war had broken out between Great Britain and Holland, which naturally affected their relations in India also and in the course of a few months led to the capture of the Dutch settlements here by the English.[3]

The terms of the proposed treaty have been described as "somewhat extravagant" even by Gleig, though he defends the measure in view of the urgent need of the English in the south of India for help in their extremely embarrassed condition.[4] There is no doubt that this proposal of Hastings was the outcome of his sincere desire to strengthen the military resources of the English at a time when their position in Southern India was surely at stake. Hastings had, indeed, his own failings in some respects. But he is certainly entitled to the gratitude of his countrymen far having made substantial contributions

1. Letter from Sir Eyre Coote, Camp New Town, dated the 1st March, 1781, to the Council in Calcutta. Proceedings, Secret Department, Fort William, 27th April, 1781.
2. Gleig, op. cit., Vol. II, pp. 336-37.
3. Proceedings, Secret Department, Fort William, 3rd July, 1781.
4. Gleig, op. cit., Vol. II, pp. 336-37.

towards the preservation of the infant British dominion in India during a critical period. His personal defence of his policy with regard to the proposed Anglo-Dutch treaty is found in one of his letters, wherein he observed :—

"You are already well acquainted with the motives of this project,. . . . I am glad that it was rejected, because the neeessity which gave birth to it has long ceased; but they should have been thankful for our endeavours however exerted, to save them, not have treated them with reproach. The measure itself was the product of their despondency, and their judgment of it the effect of that levity which little minds vibrate with every successive touch of adversity and prosperity. They had represented the Carnatic as lost; their army unable to take the field, by reason of the unconquerable dejection of the sepoys, and the reduced numbers of their European infantry. Without a great augmentation of the latter, Sir E. Coote said, he could not risk an engagement.[1] Twelve hundred European soldiers were to have been added to our army by the treaty, and a territory ceded in return which could scarcely be called our own, and which I could easily foresee would have rendered the Dutch dependent on us, had they possessed it, instead of giving them a dangerous interference, in so remote a corner, with our own possessions. But it was tuncah land, and the interests of many would have been disturbed by it. This, I believe, was the real objection. As to the ostensible ones, the first I have answered; the second is that the Dutch soldier is contemptible and would have proved of no use to us. This I deny for the best soldiers that we ever had in India have been Dutch, that is Germans, especially those who took service with us after their defeat in Colonel Forde's campaign. Their officers, indeed, are bad because they have so scanty a pay that gentlemen will not engage with them, and therefore we stipulated that we should receive none of a higher rank than Captains, and these had an honourable incentive to good behaviour in the prospect of promotion by commissions granted from our Government. A third objection is, that there was a prospect of an impending rupture with the Dutch; so much the

1. Sir Eyre Coote's letter to the Supreme Council, dated 10th November, 1780. Fort William Consultations, 14th December, 1780.

better. I am no casuist; but I belive that, in such an event their soldiers would rather continue to serve us than return to their own colours, and I certainly would not force them to leave us. We, therefore, in that case should have been doubly gainers by what we had, and what our new adversaries had thus lost."[1]

While giving Lord Marcatney, who had landed at Madras as its Governor on the 22nd June, 1781[2], description of the affairs in the Carnatic and explaining to him that it was "not from choice" but under stress of circumstances that the Calcutta government had interfered in the concerns of Madras, Hastings pointed out to him the "propriety and fairness of their (own) acts and even their necessity". He also regretfully expressed : "That which was undesirably good has been accepted as a rightful claim, the rest, as I am told either treated with derision or resented as injurious. I allude particularly to the treaty proposed with the Dutch, a measure extorted by the cries of despair, and judged in the elation of a sudden return of success.......".[3] In fact, Hastings had the desire to remain on good terms with the Dutch before the news of their joining the anti-British coalition reached India. Thus, on the complaint of J. M. Ross to the effect that Khan Jahan Khan, *faujdar* of Hugli, had sent fifty of his men to the local Dutch *thana* who arrested a *thanadar* and two *paiks* without stating any cause for this action to the *chubdar* deputed by Ross to know of it, the Governor-General ordered the *faujdar* on the 28th May, 1781, to "release the *thanadar* and *paiks* at once and despatch them to Mr. Ross and to acquaint him with the cause of their arrest".[4]

Capture of the Dutch Settlements in 1781-82

The years 1778-83 formed indeed a very critical period in the

---

1. Hastings' Letter to Scott, dated Fort William, 28th April, 1781, quoted in Gleig's Memoirs of Warren Hastings, Vol. II, pp. 356-57.
2. Mill, Vol. IV, p. 226.
3. Hastings' letter to Macartney, dated Bhagalpur, the 23rd July, 1781, quoted in Proceedings, Secret Department, Fort William, 21st July, 1783.
4. Calendar of Persian Correspondence, Vol. VI, p. 70.

history of the rising British Empire in different quarters. England was then confronted not only with the revolt of the American colonies but also with a formidable coalition of her foes in Europe. These events had undoubtedly significant repercussions on contemporary Indian politics, and particularly the attempt of France to fish in the troubled waters of India through her friendship with Hyder and Tipu, the most inveterate foes of the English in India, made the situation here also extremely critical for the British power. British reprisals were, therefore, directed against the hostile powers in all theatres of their activities including India.

In the autumn of 1780,[1] United Netherlands joined the league against England in the course of the American War of Independence. This was followed by a declaration of war by England against the Dutch on 20th December, 1780,[2] and capture of their settlements by the English. The Dutch settelments of Madras, Pulicat and Negapatam in southern India were seized by the English by the end of the year 1781[3] and Trincomali (Trincomalai) as well as Fort Ostenburg (Olenburg) belonging to them on the island of Ceylon were captured by the British fleet under the command of Admiral Sir Edward Huges on the 6th January 1782,[4] "together with a very large property in military stores and goods, also 1,50,000 dollars in specie and two India men, ready for Europe".[5]

1. Grant Robertson, Hanoverian England, p. 279.
2. Madras Dutch Record No. 13, pp. 35—37.
3. Fullarton, A View of the English Interests in India, p. 20; Mill, History of British India, Vol. IV, pp. 221—25; Thornton, History of the British Empire in India, Vol. II, p. 400.
4. We read in the works of Fullarton and Thornton that the Dutch possessions in Ceylon were captured by the end of 1781. But Mill writes that these were "taken by storm" on the 11th January, 1782 (op. cit., Vol. IV, p. 225). It is clear from a reference in Proceedings, Secret Department, Fort William, 28th February, 1782, that these were actually captured on the 6th January, 1782. Mr. Alexr. Rea (Monumental Remains of the Dutch East India Company in the Presidency of Madras, p. 30) writes that Trincomali was captured by the English in 1782; but he wrongly asserts that it was "restored to the Dutch the following year."
5. Proceedings, Secret Department, Fort William, 28th February, 1782.

The Dutch settlements in Bengal and Bihar were also captured by the English in 1781. After reaching Madras, Sir Edward Hughes sent the following instructions to Captain Parr, Commander of His Majesty's sloop the *Chaser*, on the 22nd June, 1781 : "His Majesty having been pleased to order in Council that reprisals be granted against the ships, goods and subjects of the States General of the United Provinces, so that His Majesty's ships shall and may lawfully seize all ships, vessels and goods belonging to the States General of the United Provinces or their subjects, or others inhabiting within any of the territories of the aforesaid States General and bring the same to judgment in any of the Courts of Admiralty within His Majesty's dominions, you are therefore hereby required and directed to carry into execution His Majesty's said order with the utmost of your power by taking or destroying the ships, vessels, forts, towns, goods and effects of the States General of the United Provinces, their subjects or others inhabiting within any of the territories of the aforesaid States General, and to bring the same to the judgment in any of the Courts of Admiralty within His Majesty's dominions".[1]

Captain Parr communicated to the Governor-General on the 2nd July, 1781, that Sir Edward Hughes had brought with him "despatches of consequence"[2] for the Governor-General, some of these containing "accounts of a war with the States of Holland"[3] and that he himself having received "orders to make reprisals on the Dutch" had captured four of their pilot sloops.[4] Captain Parr's letter being placed by the Governor-General before the Council in Calcutta on the 3rd July, 1781, they decided on the same date that, in view of the information it conveyed, there were sufficient grounds "for considering the war between Great Britain and the States of Holland as ascertained and declared, although not in the usual terms and forms" and that "not an instant of time ought to be lost in carrying into execution the measures consequent on this information," that is, to capture all

1. Proceedings, Secret Department, Fort William, 3rd July, 1781.
2. Ibid.
3. Ibid.
4. Ibid.

the settlements of the Dutch.

On that very day, the Council in Calcutta wrote to Captain Charles Chatfield, commanding at Chandernagore : "You are hereby directed to proceed immediately with the Force under your command to Chinsurah, to secure all the avenues of the Town both by land and by water, suffering none of the inhabitants to leave the place, nor any money, bullion or other effects to pass. Having done this you will march with a party to the Fort and demand from Mr. Ross, the Governor, the immediate surrender of it, together with the town and inhabitants. Whenever you shall have received the key of the Fort you will put Messrs. Purling, Heatly and Adair, Commissaries appointed for that purpose, into immediate possession thereof, as well as of the Town.

The Board cannot suppose that the Governor of Chinsurah will be so imprudent as to refuse obedience to the summons, having no force to enable him to offer any degree of resistance with effect, but if he should, you will in that case declare him charged with the responsibility of all the blood that may be unnecessarily spilt in consequence of such refusal and use your utmost endeavours with the Force under your command to take possession of the Fort and Town and of the effects both public and Private.

The Board recommend to you to treat the inhabitants with every degree of tenderness and that you suffer no violence to be offered than is necessary to carry these orders into execution".[1]

Each of the commanding officers at the different stations of the Army were similarly instructed to take immediate possession of the Dutch factories within their respective jurisdictions.[2] Charles Purling, S. Heatly, Robert Adair and Mr. Henry Ramus, appointed Commissaries on the part of the English Company's government to take charge of the fort and town of Chinsura, received the following orders from the Council in Calcutta on the 3rd July : "You are in the first instance to take a particular account of the Money and Bullion in the Dutch Company's Treasury and afterwards proceed to the different

1. Chandernagore and Chinsura Proceedings, 4th July to 31st December, Vol. I,—Chandernagore, the 4th July, 1781.
2. Proceedings, Secret Department, Fort William, 3rd July, 1781.

Warehouses taking an Inventory of the effect in each, and in order to accomplish this you are to require from the present governor, Mr. Ross, particular accounts of the money, bullion, goods, etc., belonging to the Dutch Company, and the assistance of their servants in their separate departments. You will likewise demand from Mr. Ross an account of the advance which have been made by the Dutch for the provision of their Company's investment, what goods have been received and what are yet to be delivered.

You will use every endeavour in your power in concert with Captain Chatfield to secure all the principal native servants of the Dutch and their accounts.

It is the particular order of the Board that you will allow the parole, agreeably to annexed form[1], to all the European inhabitants of the place of a superior order and keep the rest in close custody."[2] Further, the following circular letter was issued to the Committee of Revenue, the chiefs of the English factories of Patna, Murshidabad and Dacca, and the Resident at Balasore :—"You will therefore take inventories of all the money, bullion, and effects which may be found therein (Dutch factory), taking proper care to preserve them untouched and forward the same to the Commissaries at Chinsura, Messrs. Purling, Heatly, Adair and Ramus, with whom you will correspond, following such instructions as they may think necessary to send you for future guidance. You will allow the parole agreeable to the accompanying form to the European inhabitants of the place of a superior order and keep the rest in close custody."[3]

The Council in Calcutta regulated[4] the 'line of duty' of the Commissaries at Chinsura in the following manner :—

"First, that the Treasury Magazine, Warehouses and Storehouses of every denomination be taken charge of and sealed up by the Commissaries.

Secondly, all accounts, books, papers, etc., belonging to the

1. Vide Appendix I.
2. Proceedings, Secret Department, Fort William, 3rd July, 1781.
3. Ibid.
4. Fort William Consultations, 4th July, 1781, and Chinsura Proceedings 9th July, 1781.

Dutch Company be delivered up to the Commissaries, with an extract account of the balance in cash and of all goods and stores, which balance the Commissaries will compare with the other general accounts delivered up to them and finding it right, the Governor and Council of Chinsura shall be requested to point out where the money is lodged as also the goods and stores, they shall be examined and compared by the Commissaries who shall report whether they are found to correspond with account balance delivered in by the Governor and Council and kept under their own lock and key.

Thirdly, the Commissaries after having possessed themselves of the whole property of the Dutch Company, shall require from all individuals an exact account of their property at Chinsura, in money, goods, stores, warehouses or houses. This account shall be delivered in on oath and within a certain time; each individual shall point out where his property is lodged and if on examining the goods or money deposited in the warehouses or places sealed up by the Commissaries they shall be found to correspond with the accounts they shall be delivered up to the proprietors and applying to the Board in all difficult cases for special instruction.

Fourthly, in general, it is to be understood that private property will be secured to individuals under this express condition that a faithful account shall be given of all that belongs to the Dutch Company, whether at Chinsura or at any other part of these Provinces and also an exact account of all balances or advances made at the *aurungs* on account of the investment.

Fifthly, but before any private property be delivered up, an account thereof shall be transmitted to the Commissaries, under oath, by each individual, which account with the affidavit, shall be transmitted to the Governor-General and Council who will issue whatever orders they may think proper respecting it to the Commissaries.

Sixthly, the Commissaries shall from the books and accounts delivered over by the Governor and Council of Chinsura form an exact and distinct account of the advances made for the investment of the current year and having ascertained also the amount that was intended to be invested by the Dutch, they shall go on with the advances in the same manner as the Governor and Council of Chinsura would have done, had they remained there. The Dutch *aurungs*, for this purpose, shall be placed under the immediate charge of the Commisaries who shall appoint such persons as they may think proper or form such regulations as they may find expedient for conducting the business in such a manner that it may remain distinct and separate from all other concerns of the Company, it being the intention of the Governor-General and Council to send home the Dutch investment separate.

Seventhly, the Comissaries will make an estimate of the money that will be required for the Dutch investment, agreeable to the plan formed by the Governor and Council of Chinsura, and as it is to be paid out of the money found in Chinsura, they will reserve enough to complete it and remit to the Presidency whatever overplus may remain.

Eighthly, that for the purposes above mentioned they do inform the Board what agents and servants will be necessary, as often as they shall require the same and that they do correspond with such of the Chiefs and Collectors of the Revenue and Agents of the Board of Trade on all matters in which such correspondence shall be necessary for the due execution of their trust for which purposes orders will be issued from the Board to the former and the Board will be desired to issue the like orders to their dependants to grant them all the assistance they may be able to afford them in their several Departments.

Ninthly, that the Commissaries shall be and are empowered both jointly and separately to perform all the functions and acts above enumerated and to pass such resolutions amongst themselves as they or the majority of them shall agree upon referring all questions upon which their opinions shall be equally divided for determination to the Board and to depute any of their members wherever they shall judge it necessary for the more effectual means of ascertaining and securing the property committed to their charge.

Tenthly, that for the encouragement and reward in the execution of this trust they shall be allowed a salary to each of 500 sicca rupees per month and to draw a commission besides of ......per cent upon the net value and amount of all the money and effects of whatever denomination they shall secure and bring to account for which purpose an appraisement will be made of such stores or other things as shall not be sold or may remain for the use of the Company in such manner as the Board shall hereafter direct."

Captain Chatfield having delivered the key of the Dutch Fort at Chinsura to the Commissaries, they waited upon the Dutch Governor, John Mathias Ross. On the requisition of Ross, they supplied him with copies of '*Instructions*' and of the '*Form of Parole*' and wrote to him the following letter on the 4th July, 1781 :—"....... we request the favour of you to let us have, with as much expedition as you conveniently can,.........;an inventory of the Money, Bullion, Goods etc., belonging to the Dutch Company, supported by their accounts made up to the present day. Second, an account of the advances made by the Dutch for the provision of their Company's investment, what goods have been received and what remain to be delivered. Third a particular list of the European and other inhabitants of Chinsura, natives of Bengal, specifying those who are considered of the rank of the Gentry, and the occupations and qualities of the rest. Fourth, a list of the principal native servants of the Dutch Company, whom you will observe by our instructions we cannot permit to depart out of Chinsura..........Captain Chatfield is by his instructions to secure private, as well as, public property"[1]. In reply to this letter, Ross communicated to the Commissaries on the same day : "..........I am willing to furnish you with every point you have mentioned thereby; only I request that the article concerning private property may be taken in a more favourable sense and that every one as well Company's servants, as the other Europeans and inhabitants and the rest of the natives may enjoy the preservation of their own property, also that all the Company's servants according to their stations, may have a salary until matters betwixt the two nations may be settled in Europe."[2]

In their letter to the Governor-General and Council in Calcutta of the same date, the Commissaries informed them of all that had passed between themselves and Ross. On the 5th July, 1781, the Commissaries went into the Council Room of Ross at his request, to "hear the Parole read to the

1. Cha. Chi. Pros.—Chandernagore, 4th July, 1781.
2. Ibid.

Council and Senior Merchants of the Dutch Company."[1] They all agreed to execute it as soon as it was written out in Dutch as well as English languages. Ross promised that he would deliver the Commissaries the Parole of the Gentlemen then present and that he would let them have a list of the other Dutch servants and persons, engaged in trade, "who might be depended on for their Parole."[2] The following abstract statement of pay including perquisites, house-rent, etc., of the Dutch Company's staff at Chinsura was submitted by him to the Commissaries :—

No.	Post			Rs. as.	p.
1.	Director, or Chief at Chinsura			282-6	2/5
2.	Senior Merchants, each	94	2	188-84	
6.	Junior Merchants, each	66	12	400-8	
1.	Master Attendant			82-12	
9.	Factors, each	58	2	523-2	
3.	Factors, emoluments each	50	2	150-6	
2.	Factors, emoluments allowance per month	54	15	109-14	
2.	Officers	58	2	116-4	
1.	Do.			40-2	
6.	Book-Keepers	39	2	234-12	
12.	Assistants	34	10	415-8	
8.	Under Assistants	27	15	223-8	
5.	Assistant Surgeons	31	2	155-10	
1.	Sexton			23-2	
1.	Master Carpenter			48-8	
Total 60				Sicca rupees 2,990-10[3]	

Ross also placed before them one list of the Dutch Company's Indian servants at Chinsura and also another of the "Zamindary Servants", maintained for collecting the dues of the *Gaunges*, *Bazars* and villages dependent on the Chinsura government. Leonard Verspyck, second of the Dutch factory at Cassimbazar who had been called to Chinsura, was permitted to

1 Cha. Chi. Pros.—Chinsura, the 5th July, 1781,

2. Ibid.

3. Ibid.

return to his station after signing his parole.[1] Sebram Neaughie (Sibram Neogy), *Patwari* of the Dutch at Chinsura and Baranagore, on being asked by them to submit the *Jama Wasil* account since the last year, promised to do so soon.[2] Gopinath Roy, *diwan* of the Dutch at Chinsura, delivered to them a list[3] of the Dutch East India Company's godowns and warehouses. On the 5th July the Commissaries sent that list to Captain Charles Chatfield, and wrote to him that it was "necessary to station Guards" at the doors of all those which contained goods.[4]

As some of the Indian inhabitants of Chinsura were deserting their habitations since the surrender of the Dutch, the Commissaries issued on the 6th July, 1781, the following notice with a view to removing their apprehension and the inconvenience arising from their desertion :—

"This is to give notice to all *soudagars*, merchants, beparries, shroffs, ryots, etc., inhabitants of the village of Chinsura, in Purgunnnah Arsaf, in Chuckla Houghly, Sircar Sautgong,—that the above village belonged to the Dutch Company, but now belong to the English Company. Therefore you are all desired to remain quiet at your houses, and do your business as before and not one of you will be hurt. Those persons who run away are desired to return to their habitations, but such as do not obey this order will be deemed culpable and incur the displeasure of the Government."[5] One copy of this notice was sent to Baranagore and three copies were stuck up at the following places in the town of Chinsura,—one at the gate of the Fort, one at the Mirzapore bazar and one at the Shestamund bazar.[6]

On the 6th July, the Commissaries appointed Nanda Kumar Chakravarty, Kali Charan Bose, Ganga Narain and Govind Roy, *sircars* of the godowns and the warehouses. They wrote a letter to Captain Chatfield on the same day informing him of these appointments and requesting him to permit each one of the *sircars* to enter the warehouses, then kept under the charge of his

1. Ibid.
2. Ibid.
3. Ibid.
4. Ibid.
5. Cha. Chi. Pros.—Chinsura, the 6th July, 1781.
6. Ibid.

sepoys, "for the purpose of opening and airing them."[1] They further instructed him to issue strict orders to his sepoys "not to allow the smallest article to be carried out of them."[2] He was also requested to "order the Treasury to be opened for the purpose of taking out the Bengal accounts", though no money was to be removed therefrom without "particular notice" signified to him under their signature.[3]

Captain Chatfield did not express his willingness to comply unconditionally with the instructions of the Commissaries. He wrote to them in reply on the 6th July : "I hereby protest against being answerable for any goods or treasure in the Dutch Company's Godowns or in the Godowns of private merchants unless before they shall be opened you give me a particular account of what is in each godown."[4] In his second letter to them written on the same date, he added : "As the accompanying letter is couched in the style of orders, which I know of no authority you have to give me, I therefore beg you will alter it. I am ready to comply with any request you may make for the good of the service".[5] Immediately on receipt of these letters the Commissaries wrote to Mr. Chatfield : "We have received your letter of this date. It is impossible for us to fix the degree of responsibility, which you may think rests upon you. The Board will determine upon this point upon being informed of our measures, and that your sepoys are placed at the doors of every one of the public Warehouses. We request you will be pleased to give the orders to your officers and sepoys we have desired of you in our last......We have just received your letter enclosing the first we addressed you, which you say you return because couched in the style of orders and beg we will alter it. We are at a loss to conceive what part of our letter is in an improper style and we cannot think of committing ourselves so far in the attention of our letter as to make a tacit declaration of the impropriety you seem to point at. We think it scarcely possible, you can believe, we mean

1. Ibid.
2. Ibid.
3. Ibid.
4. Ibid.
5. Ibid.

to make any request of you, incompatible with the good of that service you know to be entrusted to our Commission."[1] The Commissaries also referred their correspondence with Chatfield to the Governor-General and Supreme Council in Calcutta requesting them "to have such a line drawn for the conduct" of the officer commanding at Chinsura "as to the requisition which they may be under the necessity of making from time to time as to place them beyond the possibility of altercation and cavil."[2]

At a meeting of the Commissaries, held on the 9th July, 1781, they thought it advisable to defer the examination of 'public property' till they had received the accounts of the Dutch from John Mathias Ross, the Dutch Director at Hugli.[3] So they transmitted to him on that day an extract of the instructions of the Governor-General and Council in Calcutta on the subject of their taking charge of 'public property' and requested him in a letter to inform all members of the Dutch Council, and also others dependent on the Dutch, that they required "the accounts of their respective property within one month from that date" agreeable to the form above prescribed and specifying the amount in cash, quantity of their goods and the places where they are lodged.[4] For private property, the Commissaries decided that the regulations regarding it should be made known to the inhabitants of Chinsura so that each of them might prepare the account of his property in the prescribed form without delay. They accordingly issued a notice in that town asking its inhabitants "to deliver in just accounts of their property" to the Commissaries on the part of the English Government in Chinsura. in the course of one month.[5]

On the 11th July, 1781, John Mathias Ross sent to the Commissaries at Chinsura the following reply to their letter to him of the 9th July : "......the difficulties which will arise by the Regulations contained in the said your favour and the diversity of opinions in what manner to execute them best, have

1. Ibid.
2. Ibid.
3. Chinsura Proceedings, 9th July, 1781.
4. Ibid.
5. Ibid.

occasioned the following remarks which I beg leave to refer to your judgment. It appears to me that the order given by your Government to inventory all private property, is only intended to prevent any concealment of the Company's goods....I have repeated this afterwards to you that not a single rupee nor pound of the Company's goods would be concealed; afterwards I have together with all the Gentlemen who had any administration of the Company's effects signed our parole of honor and what is contained in that paper I need not to repeat. I have given the most strict orders for closing the Company's books especially in conformity with your request the accounts of the cash which would surely have been ready at this time if the administrator had been able to get the necessary papers for the purpose which were deposited there and which were absolutely wanted to give you an accurate account of the balance which the bengalys (Bengalis) or their papers could by no means give you, as according to our constitution they have no further management of any affairs as is absolutely necessary to transact business with their countrymen.—As speedy as this business is done (which is an affair of much importance and which requires the strictest exactness cannot be done on a sudden), I will deliver you the most exact accounts of every article which belongs to the Company and which being compared with the books and other accounts and the balances of money and goods will leave no doubt for any deceiving. And now Gentlemen having requested your particular attention on this point I conclude in testifying you my most hearty wishes that it would please you to point out such expedient means as in a short time may surmount all difficulties and regulate everything to our mutual satisfaction as I am fearful that a continual correspondence and representation on both sides might occasion confusion, will spend more time than is required and perhaps give rise to altercation which I anxiously wish to avoid."[1] In reply the Commissaries wrote him as follows on the 13th July: "We have been honoured with your letter of the 11th. On the third paragraph of which we beg leave to recur to our letter of the 9th concerning private property. We understand that individuals will be secured therein if a faithful

1. Ibid.

account is rendered of the affairs of the Dutch Company at Chinsura and within the Provinces and that individuals are required to deliver to us faithful and exact accounts upon oath of their property whether at Chinsura or in any part of the Provinces and we are directed to compare these accounts with the effects thus specified and refer them for the orders of our superior. Nothing, Sir, but a misrepresentation of our intentions which are with every deference to and consideration for your nation a desire punctually to adhere to the orders of our Government can lead to the altercation you express yourself so desirous of avoiding. We shall ever find a pleasure in giving you such satisfaction as we find we are competent to do, and will with readiness refer such points for the ultimate decision of the Hon'ble Governor-General and Council as we have not explicit instructions on."[1]

As provided by the article 6 of the Regulations drawn by the Governor-General and Council in Calcutta for the conduct of the Commissaries, the latter appointed Mr. Patrick Heatly, Mr. John Craigie, and Mr. Samuel Hasleby their Deputies to take charge of the Dutch factories at Patna, Cassimbazar and Dacca respectively.[2] Messrs. William Maxwell, William Hosia and William Holland, Revenue Chiefs at Patna, Murshidabad and Dacca respectively, were requested by the English Commissaries at Chinsura to render all possible assistance to their Deputies in the discharge of their duties[3]. Similar requests were made by them to Messrs. Edward Stephenson, Simeon Droze and Henry Cottrell, Commercial Chiefs at Patna, Cassimbazar and Dacca respectively[4]. Mr. Patrick Heatly (employed in the Revenue Accountant-General's office in Calcutta) was then informed of his new appointment and furnished with the following instruc-

1. Ibid.
2. Ibid, Mr. Samuel Hasleby was previously employed under the Board of Trade in Calcutta. Letter from the Board of Trade in Calcutta to the Commissaries at Chinsura, dated 17th July, 1781,—quoted in Chinsura Proceedings, 21st July, 1781. Mr. John Craigie held the post of surgeon to the Commercial Department at Cassimbazar. Letter from the Commissaries at Chinsura to the Governor-General and Council in Calcutta, quoted in Chinsura Proceedings, 21st July, 1781.
3. Chinsura Proceedings, 9th July, 1781.
4. Ibid.

tions by the Commissaries : "..You will proceed with all the expedition you can make..you will apply to the person who may now be in charge of the Dutch Factory at Patna to deliver over to you the keys and possessions of the above Factory and of the Treasury, Magazines, Warehouses, Store houses, of every denomination. You will also require of the Dutch chief all the accounts belonging to the Dutch Company to be given up to you with an extract account of the balance of cash in hand and of all the goods and stores in the Dutch Treasury and Warehouses. An inventory whereof you will transmit to us with all the expedition in your power. The private property in general you will understand will be secured to individuals under the Dutch protection at Patna under the express condition that a faithful account shall be rendered of all that belongs to the Dutch Company at that place or any part dependent thereupon and also an exact account of all balances or advances made on account of their investment; but before any private property shall be delivered up, an account thereof shall be given to you under oath by every individual specifying the amount of cash or goods in what places deposited and also their houses, warehouses, etc. The property itself to be compared by you with the account delivered in and transmitted to us that we may submit them to the Hon'ble Governor-General and Council for such orders as they may think proper to issue thereupon. You will transmit us a list of all the servants of the Dutch East India Company employed in their Factory, specifying their names, stations or employments and qualities....You will request the assistance of the native Dutch Company's servants a list of whom you will require of the Dutch Chief and you will from time to time inform us what further servants may be nceessary for the transaction of your business."[1] Mr. Philip Milner Dacres, President of the Commercial Council in Calcutta, was requested by the Commissaries at Chinsura to spare the services of Mr. Samuel Hasleby to enable him to act as their Deputy at Dacca.[2]

On the 6th July, 1781, the Council in Calcutta had decided to issue following advertisment : "Whereas it has been long un-

1. Ibid.
2. Ibid.

derstood by the Members of this Government, that the servants of the Company and others have been, for some time past, accustomed to receive Commissions for the Provisions of the Investment of the Dutch Company in these Provinces, all such persons who shall have received advances of Money from the Director and Council of Chinsura or shall have entered into any Engagements or Contracts with them for the Provision of the Investment of the Dutch Company, or shall have any other Dealings with the Dutch Government, or any Members of it, on account of the Dutch East India Company, are hereby called upon and required to give a true and faithful account of the same to Messrs. Purling, Heatly, Adair and Ramus, appointed Commissaries for the immediate charge of the United States; and either to deliver over to the said Commissaries all the money, goods and accounts of the Dutch Company in their charge, or to continue in the charge and Execution of the said Commission, Engagements or Contracts; and to obey all such instruction as they shall receive from the said Commissaries concerning the same; and to receive such further advances as may be necessary for completing Commissions with which they may have been originally entrusted by the Directors or Chiefs of the Dutch Company; or for fulfilling such Engagements or Contracts as they may have entered into with them."[1] Twelve copies of it were sent to the Commissaries at Chinsura for its circulation among the persons concerned and on the 13th July they decided to act accordingly.[2]

In conformity with the orders of the Council in Calcutta, dated the 8th July, 1781, the Commissaries supplied Colonel Henry Watson, Commander of a vessel, with such masts, spars, cables, etc., as were necessary for the equipments of his vessel.[3] Mr. W. Paxton, Mint-Master in Calcutta, had sent on the 11th July, 1781, his *sarkar* Ramkanai to the Commissaries at Chinsura to purchase there five maunds of Japan copper for the use of the English Company's mint in Calcutta.[4] Ramkanai was permitted

1. Chinsura Proceedings, dated 13th July, 1781.
2. Ibid.
3. Ibid.
4. Ibid.

by them to transport to Calcutta the requisite quantity of copper on the 13th July[1]. On the 14th July, the Commissaries sent to the Council in Calcutta four chests of ingots of gold, found in the Dutch Factory at Chinsura[2]. At the request of his colleagues, Mr. Charles Purling formally took charge of the Dutch treasury at Chinsura on the 17th July, and found there in cash sicca rupees 2,33,282-5-3.[3]

There were thirty-six Dutch prisoners in the Fort William in Calcutta. Lieutenant P. Arnold undertook "to procure the provisions" for them. The Commissaries at Chinsura wrote to Lieutenant Arnold on the 14th July, 1781, requesting him "to make out a monthly estimate of the expense and correspond with them on all matters relative to this business."[4] The Dutch prisoners in Fort William informed J. M. Ross on the 13th July, 1781, that the Captain of the ship Chaser had asked them to remain in readiness for being transported on his vessel to Madras. J. M. Ross thereupon addressed the following letter to the Commissaries at Chinsura on the 14th July: "As all of these people have their houses, Wives, and Children here in Chinsura, I cannot help lamenting the hardness of their fate, should this order be executed and they all on a sudden be deprived of all their property and what must be more dear to them their Wives and Children. Humanity as well as the obligation I am under to take care for them as good subjects oblige me therefore to take their Interest at Heart. And on this principle I beg leave most friendly to solicit your friendly offices in their behalf that the abovementioned order may not be executed to them, but that they may stay where they are or if possible that the favour may be shown to them to be kept prisoners here amongst their families."[5] A copy of this letter was immediately sent by the Commissaries to the Governor-General and Council in Calcutta for their consideration.[6] What happened of the prisoners after this is not known to us.

1. Ibid.
2. Chinsura Proceedings, 14th July, 1781.
3. Chinsura Proceedings, 17th July, 1781.
4. Ibid.
5. Ibid.
6. Ibid.

After the capture of Chinsura by the English many of its Dutch inhabitants were reduced to plight. Sir Robert Chambers, who had been sent there as superintendent of the Courts of Justice, represented to the Governor-General in Calcutta that many of them "being deprived of their former means of subsistence were reduced to the greatest indigence, and several of the more respectable families brought to such distress as to be obliged privately to sell their furniture and ornaments to maintain themselves". At this the Governor-General in Council decided to spend a portion of the revenues of that town for the support of these poor inhabitants "under the direction and discretion" of Sir Robert Chambers, who was instructed to "relieve more privately the wants of these families who might be degraded by the receipt of public charity".[1]

The Dutch possession of Baranagore was also at the same time captured by the English. Directed by the Governor-General and Council in Calcutta to "take charge of the stores and effects both public and private belonging to the Dutch Factory at Baranagore", the Committee of Revenue in Calcutta deputed John David Paterson on this business on the 6th July, 1781.[2] Paterson took charge of the effects of the Dutch at Baranagore from Sergeant Major Beniva, who "commanded the detachment"[3] and sent an inventory of these to the Committee of Revenue. The Committee of Revenue while sending to the Commissaries at Chinsura copy of a letter to it from Mr. Paterson, containing an inventory of the articles which came into his possession, wrote to them on the 13th July, 1781: "We have directed him (Mr. Paterson) to keep possession of articles for the present till you shall depute some person to take charge of them, when they will be delivered up on your sending us the necessary

---

1. Letter to Court, 9th May, 1782, para 18 D.
Robert Chambers joined the Calcutta Supreme Court as second Judge in 1774. He was one of the Judges in the case of Nanda Kumar. He was appointed Chief Justice and President of the Chinsura Court of Justice in 1780 and Chief Justice of the Calcutta High Court in 1791.
2. Letter from the Committee of Revenue, dated Calcutta 13th July, 1781, to the Commissaries at Chinsura, Chinsura Proceedings, 17th July, 1781.
3. Ibid.

information. As we have received no authority from the Governor-General and Council to collect the rents of Baranagore we think it necessary to mention this for your information that you may take measures for securing them"[1]. John Craigie, appointed Deputy on behalf of the Commissaries at Chinsura for the Dutch Factory at Kalikapore (near Cassimbazar in the Murshidabad district), received "charge and possession" of the said factory from the acting Chief of Murshidabad on the 18th July, 1781[2]. He informed the Commissaries of it on the same date and assured them that he "shall forthwith proceed to the execution of their orders with all possible despatch."[3]

---

1. Ibid.
2. Chinsura Proceedings, 21st July, 1781.
3. Ibid.

CHAPTER VI

Dutch Settlements, 1784-1816

Restoration of Settlements after Versailles

The year 1783 marked the close of a period of acute international rivalries among the western powers. A treaty of peace and friendship between England and France was signed at Versailles on the 3rd September, 1783, which was soon followed by one between England and Holland. These provided for the mutual restitution of conquests by the English, the French and the Dutch. But the mutual restoration of conquered territories in India was not effected immediately after the news of the pacification in Europe had reached here. The Dutch governments at Colombo and Batavia complained to the Council in Calcutta against this delay, caused particularly by difference of opinion between the Madras Government and the representatives of the French in India about the cession of Trincomali to the Dutch[1]. Mr. Hastings observed in his Minute, dated the 16th. November, 1784:—

"........That, as by the scrupulous Adherence of the President and Select Committee of Fort St. George to the Letter of the Treaties concluded by Great Britain with France and Holland, both the Letter and spirit of those Treaties have been defeated and have been suffered by the President and Select Committee to remain unaccomplished to a long and indefinite period. As our Nation acquires no Advantage whatsoever by the Delay; but the French retain possession of every conquest made by them from us, together with the real and substantial possession of Pondicherry and the absolute possession of Trincomali. As the Dutch complain, and have a just plea to complain, that

---

1. We have already noted how Trincomali was captured by the English. Sir Edward Hughes had to surrender it to the French fleet under Mons. Suffrein on the last day of August, 1782 (Mill, Vol. IV, p. 253). The immediate efforts of Sir Edward Hughes to recover it proved to be of no avail. Letter of Sir Edward Hughes to Lord Macartney, dated 8th September, 1782. Proceedings, Secret Department, Fort William, 23rd September, 1782. (Vide Appendix J)

the suspension, which is in effect a direct violation of the Treaty concluded with their nation, is imputable solely to our Perseverence in demanding what the Murquis de Bussy, the Representative of the French Crown, has no authority to yield and is commanded not to yield. As the point on which the President and Select Committee of Fort St. George have with much vehemence and firmness of Perseverence insisted, is only to be put in possession of the fort and territory of Trincomali, previously to its cession to the Dutch, and for the purpose of enabling them to make the cession. As the only reason for insisting on this point is founded on the Right of the Dutch to actual possession, which if left to the discretion of the Government of France, might be frustrated. As the Dutch have themselves waived their claim to this attention on our part to their Rights and desire to receive possession immediately from the French agents. As the Treaties themselves stipulate that all the cessions shall be made in the same epoch, which expression whether it be construed period or Point of time, equally entitles Dutch Company to immediate possession......As the adherence of the Representative of our Nation to the claim of being put in possession of Trincomali, no Treaty in term requiring it, may furnish, if not a suspicion, at least a Pretext to alledge it, of an Intention on our part to keep possession after it shall be obtained, and may thereby furnish a just Agreement for the French to withhold it entirely. As it can not fail to impress the Natives of India with a false opinion of the Decline of the British Power, to see the French, its great rival, after the close up of a desperate war, retain all the conquests made on our Nation, with all but former possession, which in effect is none, of those, which had been made by us on them. And finally, as the Faith and Honour of our Nation, which have been rendered liable to imputation by this unprofitable contention, have been now made to depend for their Preservation on this Government by the References made to it. The Governor-General recommends in the spirit of the propositions referred to him that a letter be immediately written to the Marquis de Bussy, both requiring him in terms of his instructions to deliver up the Fort of Trincomale and its dependencies to the Representatives of the Dutch Government of Colombo; and empowering him to constitute such Agents as he may think proper to perform so much of this process as may be construed to appertain formally to the representatives of our Nation; and at the same time to require him to deliver over the Fort, Town and Districts of Cuddalore to such Agents as shall be deputed for that purpose to receive the same from the President and Select Committee of Fort Saint George......".[1]

The Governor-General's Minute received the approval of the other members of the Council in Calcutta, and on the 23rd November, 1784, the Council wrote a letter to Marquis de Bussy, Commander-in-Chief of the French Forces in India by Sea and Land, on the basis of its proposition.[2] On the same day the Council in Calcutta wrote to the Batavia government[3] and the Dutch Council at Colombo informing them of the abovementioned communication to Bussy and of their intention to give full effect to the terms of the treaty as soon as possible. Though inclined to let the Dutch have immediate possession of their captured settlements[4], they could not formally restore Chinsura to them as the relevant article of the preliminaries of the Treaty between Great Britain and the Netherlands provided that restitutions and evacuations of territories between them should take place "at the same periods" as those between Great Britain and France. But in view of the delay "in the execution of the stipulation of the Treaties", the Council in Calcutta "thought proper to deliver over to the Chief and Council at Chinsura, the warehouses and factories belonging to the Dutch at that place, Cassimbazar and Patna and Baranagore (near Calcutta) and to permit them to land their goods and to establish their own laws and such regulations as they may think proper in Chinsura, in every point except that of hoisting their colours in that place or introducing troops or Military stores" which they could not allow until they had heard of "the Execution of the Definitive Treaty" on the part of Marquis de Bussy.[5] Necessary instructions were, at the same time,

1. Foreign Dept. Proceedings, 23rd November, 1784.
2. Vide Appendix, K.
3. Vide Appendix, L.
4. Letter from the Council in Calcutta to the Council at Fort St. George, 23rd November, 1784.
5. Foreign Department Proceedings, 23rd November, 1784; Letter to Court, 8th December, 1784, paras 7-9.

sent to the Councils at Fort St. George and Bombay for due execution of the terms of the treaties in their respective jurisdictions as soon as Bussy had agreed to the propositions communicated to him.

The Dutch Chief and Council at Chinsura appreciated this policy of the Council in Calcutta and "allowed full weight to the reasons that operated with the latter" against a more perfect compliance for the present with the applications received from Batavia."[1] When Trincomali was finally restored to the Dutch in April, 1784, the Council of the Dutch at Colombo wrote to the Council in Calcutta expressing satisfaction at this and also for readily delivering up Chinsura to their representatives. The Dutch factory at Surat and their settlements on the Coromandel coast were also soon restored to them[2].

When the Dutch wanted permission for hoisting their flag at Chinsura, the English granted it reserving to themselves, however, "the right of withdrawing it when any case should occur to make this" their "indispensable duty"[3]. But the Dutch were not satisfied at this. "They appear to claim rather as a Right", wrote the Council in Calcutta to the Court of Directors, on the 14th January, 1784, "what was before solicited merely as a favour, and, instead of candidly accepting what we had done, they indirectly reproach us for not having done more"[4].

There were occasionally some minor differences between the Dutch and the English. But these were soon accommodated. The Commissioners of Customs of the English East India Company complained to their masters that when the Collector of Customs at Hugli demanded from Herklots, the Dutch Chief at Chinsura, satisfactory vouchers for the quantity and variety of goods imported by each slop of the Dutch, he "under various pretences and from time to time, refused to deliver them"[5]. For this the Dutch ship Straaten was detained by the Collector of Government Customs of the English East India Company. But when the Dutch complained about it to the Council in Calcutta

1. Ibid.
2. Letter to Court, 31st July, 1785, paras 29-38.
3: Letter to Court, 17th January, 1785, para 3.
4. Ibid, para 7.
5. Ibid, para 7.

the latter "issued orders to the Board of Customs to release a Boat that was said to be yet Detained and to permit all such other Boats to pass as the gentlemen at Chinsura might Dispatch to the Straaten, relying on their report, or on that of the persons in charge of the Boats, for a true Account of the quantity of each Cargo, that the Amount of Duties to be collected, if any, might be ascertained hereafter"[1]. The Council in Calcutta showed, as they claimed, "an earnest Inclination to cultivate and improve that good understanding" which had been lately revived between England and Holland. Identity of interests led both to maintain good relations.

It is interesting to note that the English in India had already, in the course of the last few months, received some assistance from the Dutch at Batavia. The Council in Calcutta stated in one of their letters to the Council at Batavia, dated the 23rd November, 1784 :—

"..... We beg leave to assure you that we are truly sensible of the favourable attention which you have shewn to the Request contained in our letter of the 15th of December, 1783, in permitting a supply of rice to be sent from Batavia for the Relief of the Carnatic; a kindness enhanced in the value of it by the state of your own wants and the other circumstances which you have recited to us.

We have been informed by the President and Council at Fort St. George that no invoice accompanied the rice which you did us the favour to embark in the Vansittart. They have however transmitted to us an account of the quantity actually landed at Madras, and we have the Honour to enclose a copy of it.

We propose to furnish the Chief and Council at Chinsura with another Transcript of it, and as there are some charges to be paid by this Government, the amount of which we cannot exactly ascertain, we mean to request that the gentlemen at Chinsura will be pleased to propose an account of what may be due to your nation for the Grain, that we may know our exact debt which will be discharged partly in money and partly in Salt Petre, agreeably to your desire"[2].

---

1. Ibid, para 8.
2. Foreign Department Proceedings, 23rd November, 1784.

The Dutch Factory at Balasore and Anglo-Dutch differences there in 1786-87

The Dutch did not immediately get back all their settlements. The factory at Balasore remained in possession of the English from its capture by them in 1781 till January, 1786. Lawrence D' Costa, Agent of the Dutch at their Balasore Factory, wrote two letters to[1] Isaac Titsingh, Governor of the Council at Chinsura, on the 23rd October, 1787 and the 10th October, 1788, complaining against Wordsworth, Resident of the English Factory at Balasore, regarding the obstructions the latter had put on his trade in *Cowries* (small glossy shells) with the Maldivians (traders from Maldives), who frequented the port of Balasore, and for his mal-treatment of the local Dutch servants and dependants. Lawrence D' Costa observed that it was not possible to get his grievances redressed by the Maratha Government in Orissa, as "here in the Maharatta Durbar they do notice only to those who bribe them"[2].

Titsingh forwarded these letters to Lord Cornawallis, Governor-General in Calcutta, soliciting redress of the Dutch Agent's grievances. The Governor-General placed these before the members of the Council in Calcutta for their joint consideration on the 12th January, 1789, and proposed that their copies be transmitted to Wordsworth with orders to communicate to the Council the nature of the trade in *cowries*[3], which had given rise to the differences between him and the Dutch Agent, and to answer the several charges levelled against him by the latter for acts of violence which he was "therein accused of having committed in order to exclude Mr. D' Costa from a share in the Trade in *Cowries* with the Maldivians"[4].

The Council in Calcutta wrote to Titsingh on the 12th January, 1789, that they would duly consider his complaints as soon as they had received Wordsworth's answers on them. The conduct of the Council in Calcutta on this occasion was

1. Appendix M.
2. It is indeed a highly poignant but well deserved comment on the debased character of later Maratha administration.
3. Vide Appendix N.
4. Foreign Department Proceedings, 12th January, 1789.

quite in consonance with the friendly relation then existing between England and the Government of the Netherlands, particularly after the Triple Alliance of 1788 between England, Prussia and Holland and the Anglo-Dutch defensive alliance (April, 1788).

Exchange of the Dutch Settlement of Baranagore for some lands in the vicinity of Hugli

Baranagore, situated about six miles north of Calcutta, was an old and important settlement of the Dutch in India[1]. Out of several important considerations, the Dutch decided, during the administration of Warren Hastings, to have it exchanged with the English for some lands near Hugli. The concluding paragraph of the Memorial of the Dutch to Warren Hastings and the Council in Calcutta, dated the 10th April, 1775, contained the following proposal : "The village of Bernagore (Baranagore) lying in the neighbourhood of Calcutta and thus very advantageous for your settlement, we tender to you in Exchange by way of Barter for as much ground in the Circle or Environs of Chinsurah as Baraneggar contain its full extent. On account of its great distance from us, and have by no particular Person to govern them; the possession of it is of the less consequence to us but of the greater importance to your Honours, on account of its aforesaid vicinity. You will therefore be pleased to take this proposal into consideration, and if it can with consistence, suffer it to take place."[2]

The Government of Warren Hastings was in 'favour of this exchange on the ground of "the mutual advantage expected to result therefrom to the Parties"[3]. So the Calcutta Committee of Revenue deputed Perring in December, 1777, to ascertain the extent and value of the town and environs of Baranagore,

1. The Diaries of Streynsham Master (edited by Sir R. C. Temple), Vol. I, p. 324 and Vol. II, p. 240 ; Hedges Diary (Hakluyt Publication), Vol. I, p. 174 and Vol. III, p. ccxvi.
2. Secret Consultations, 25th April, 1775, No. 2. Vide proceedings of the Indian Historical Records Commission, 18th Session (Mysore).
3. Foreign Department Proceedings, 12th January, 1789.

and of the land near Hugli which the Dutch proposed to receive in exchange thereof.[1] Perring submitted a report on the 30th April, 1778.[2] It appears from the procedings of the Governor-General and Council, dated the 7th January, 1779, that the "Sudder Jumma or net annual rent of the Dutch possessions at Baranagore exclusive of the collections or duties on Hauts or Bazars (marketplaces) an account of which could not then be procured, mounted to Sicca Rupees 1,961-13-0 and that the Sudder Jumma of the ground lying contiguous to Hougley (Hugli), which the Dutch had pointed out as Lands to be given in exchange for Baranagore, amouted to Rs. 3,938-7-3 (sic) from which the sum of Rs. 1,200-15-10 amount the head of Sayer[3] collections, also omitted in the Branagore estimate being deducted there remains a net Revenue of Rupees 2,737-9-17-3 (sic). This sum exceeding the value of Baranagore in the amount of Rs. 775-12-17-3" (sic). The Calcutta government, therefore, proposed to the Director and Council at Chinsura "either to assign over to them a specific proportion of the said Lands equivalent to the value of Baranagore, or to transfer to them the whole quantity upon condition of their paying ten years' Purchase for the above surplus, that is rupees 1,758 or an annual rent to Government for the possession of it equal to the amount of the Settlement."[4] But at this stage negotiations for the exchange were abruptly broken off by the Dutch Council at Chinsura on the ground that their authorities at Batavia "had not given their final sanction to the measure".[5]

Again during the administration of Lord Cornwallis, Isaac Titsing, the Dutch Director at Chinsura, expressed, in the course of an interview with him, the desire to renew the negotiations for the exchange of Baranagore for some lands in the vicinity of Hugli.[6] Lord Cornwallis observed before the Council in Calcutta on the 12th January 1789 : "......the proposed exchange is not only advantageous for the Dutch but in every res-

1. Ibid.
2. Ibid.
3. Vide Glossary.
4. Foreign Department Proceedings, 12th January, 1789.
5. Ibid.
6. Ibid.

pect desirable for this (English Company's) Government. Being contiguous to the Town of Calcutta and under a Foreign jurisdiction it affords a shelter to disorderly people, and should the Dutch think proper to assume the exercise of the same national privileges at Bernagore (Baranagore) as they possess at Chinsurah many political inconveniences would result therefrom to this Government."[1] He, therefore, proposed the acceptance of Titsingh's offer, and, as a preliminary step, the Board of Revenue in Calcutta was called upon, at his suggestion, to report to the Council in Calcutta "whether since the period at which Mr. Perring's estimate of the Revenues from the lands contiguous to Houghly (Hugli), as pointed out by the Director and Council at Chinsura, was made, any, and if any, what alterations have taken place in the Jumma of those lands" and whether they were "aware of any objections to the whole or part of them being made over to the Dutch in the manner originally proposed in exchange for their possessions at Bernagore".[2] At the same time the Council in Calcutta informed the Dutch Directorate at Chinsura that, "considering such an exchange as convenient to both parties", they were prepared to effect it as soon as the latter had intimated to them that they were "ready to proceed upon it".[3]

In 1792 Titsingh, Director of the Dutch Company at Chinsura, was permitted by his authorities to resign this office and got a seat in the Dutch Supreme Council of Batavia. Cornelius Van Citters Aunaietoz was appointed his successor at Chinsura. The Dutch Council at Chinsura due to "great want of resources to enable them to carry on the affairs of their Company in Bengal, not having received some expected supplies from Batavia"[4] earnestly requested the Council in Calcutta to help them with a loan of a lac of rupees for bills on their Governor-General and Council at Batavia. The Council in Calcutta agreed to grant this loan on the condition that the amount of the loan was repaid into the treasury of the English supercargoes at Can-

1. Ibid.
2. Ibid.
3. Ibid.
4. Letter to Court, 3rd September, 1792, paras 12-17.

ton, sometime between the 1st of November, 1792, and the 31st of January, 1793, and at the exchange of fortyone dollars for one hundred current rupees. Bills on the terms suggested by the Council in Calcutta were given to them by the Dutch Council of Chinsura and to facilitate early action, the former approved of the suggestions of Titsingh that these should be carried by him to Batavia for forwarding these to the English Supercargoes at Canton soon after his arrival at Batavia. The Dutch Supreme Council at Batavia sent orders to their Supercargoes to pay the amount of the loan to the English Supercargoes at Canton.

Most probably the exchange took place in 1795.[1] The first article of the Convention, concluded between His Majesty the King of England and Government of the Netherlands on the 13th of August, 1814, stipulated that "all the Colonies, Factories and Establishments, which were in the Seas and on the continents of America, Africa and Asia with certain exceptions specified, be restored to that Dutch power".[2] Such exceptions were made with regard to Cochin and Baranagore.[3]

Dutch Settlements under British Protection

France declared war against England and Holland on the 1st February, 1793. This news reached India from the British Consul at Alexandria on the 1st June, 1793. While communicating it to the Duch Director at Chinsura the Governor-General in Calcutta gave him the following assurance of their friendship : "It can hardly be supposed that the people at Chandernagore, although they may receive early intelligence of this event, will venture to molest the settlement at Chinsurah; but, in that or any other case, you may be entirely certain that the friendship and alliance subsisting between our Governments will secure to you every assistance from us that you may require".[4] In a conference of the Governor-General with Hanguitz of the Dutch Council

---

1. Twentyfour-Parganas District Gazetteer, p. 215.
2. Fort William Consultations, 17th December, 1816, No. 2.
3. Ibid.
4. Letters to Court, 1st August, 1793, para 13;
   13th August, 1793, para 33.

at Chinsura he agreed to comply with a request of the Dutch Council at Chinsura to lend them 63,000 sicca rupees free of interest, for purchasing sufficient quantity of rice to be transported by them to the Dutch at Colombo. The Dutch were, however, required to make repayment of it to the Council in Calcutta as the latter considered that it "would be highly inconvenient to them to receive bills of exchange on Batavia".[1]

Towards the close of the year 1794, the French overran the whole of Holland, and occupied Amsterdam in January, 1795. The Stadholder fled to England, and a Batavian republic, dependent on France, was soon declared. The Stadholder being obliged to take refuge in England, the Government of His Brittanic Majesty decided to bring all Dutch possessions in the East under their control probably with a view to preventing their utilisation by the pro-French powers in India for anti-British activities. A proclamation[2] was accordingly issued to the Government of the Dutch Settlements in the East Indies demanding the transfer of all these to the possession of the English until the restoration of the old government in Holland after a 'general pacification' in Europe. They were assured therein that, during that period, their settlements would be entitled to "advantages, privileges and immunities" similar to those enjoyed by the English Settlements in the East Indies.

In February, 1795, the fugitive Prince issued a circular exhorting his late subjects "to place their colonies under the protection of Great Britain"[3]. In accordance with this the Council in Calcutta deputed Birch, who was Superintendent of Chandernagore after its capture by the English in July, 1795, to take possession of Chinsura, with the help of a military force, if necessary.[4] He was appointed Commissioner of Chinsura and its dependencies, and was instructed to take "care that no sort of violence be offered to any of the inhabitants and that no property, public or private, be in any shape molested or interfered, with". It was declared

---

1. Letter to Court, 15th May, 1794, paras 6-8.
2. Appendix O.
3. Madras Dutch Record No. 13, p. 38
4. The Governor-General's Minute, dated 21st July, 1795; Secret Consultations, 24th July, 1795, No. 6.

that it was not the intention of the English "to interfere in any respect with their (of the Dutch) internal administration further than to leave (at Chinsura) a small guard for the protection of the British flag"[1]. The English Government in Calcutta also ordered H. Douglas, Judge and Magistrate of Patna, on the 14th August, 1795, to occupy the Dutch factory there on the terms of the above-mentioned proclamation.[2] In case of resistance from the local Dutch Chief, he was authorised to take military assistance from the Commanding Officer at Dinapore to take possession of the Dutch factory. He was, however, instructed to be very particular about treating the inhabitants with "attention and kindness" and to let them (Dutch subjects) know that their laws and customs shall not be infringed upon, that they will not be subject to the payment of fresh taxes or duties, and that they will be permitted "to trade to and from the English Company's Settlements with the same advantages as the subjects" of the English nation.[3] The Magistrate at Murshidabad was ordered to take possession of the Dutch factory at Kalkapur. The Dutch settlements on the east and west coasts of India also came under the influence of the English in the same year.[4] Franco-Dutch alliance then caused much uneasiness to the Company's Government in India and "the rumour that a powerful Dutch fleet was at sea destined to co-operate with the French, deepened the alarm."[5] But Sir George Kelth Elphinstone met the Dutch fleet at Cape of Good Hope and forced it to surrender "relieving the Government of India of all fear from that of water."[6]

The peace of Amiens, signed on the 27th March, 1802, provided that England should retain of her conquests only Ceylon and Trinidad, the rest being restored to France or allies of France. Soon after this, Lord Wellesley got orders from the

1. Ibid.
2. Patna District Judge Court Records.
3. Appendix P.
4. Monumental Remains of the Dutch East India Company in the Presidency of Madras, pp 330—37; Thornton, History of the British Empire in India, Vol. II, p. 558 and Vol. III, p. 388; Secret Letters to Court, 18th August, 1795, para 19; 31st October, 1795, para 21 D.
5. Nolan, The History of the British Empire in India and the East, p. 464.
6. Ibid.

Home Government to give back to the French and Batavian Republics all their settlements in India excepting the Dutch ports in Ceylon. But French influence still continued to be predominant in different parts of Europe. "Look", observed Sheridan a year later, "at the map of Europe. You will see nothing but France". Napolean proudly remarked, "It is recognised in Europe that Italy, Holland and Switzerland, are at the disposal of France". There could be no doubt about French designs also in the East. The political aims of Napoleon and England were still too conflicting to allow a lasting peace. Lord Hawkesbury, Foreign Secretary of England in the Cabinet of Henry Addington, sent intelligence to Lord Wellesley about the impending recrudescence of hostilities with France and Holland. On getting this information, the Governor-General in India "regulated all his proceedings upon the assumed certainty of war with France and Holland".[1] He had not restored to the French and the Dutch their settlements in India, which continued under the control of the English till the close of the Napoleonic Wars. On the death of Sohnlein, Chief the Dutch Factory at Patna, in May, 1803, his effects were sent by Henry Douglas, Judge-Magistrate of Patna,[2] to his executors Bowman of Chinsura and Ullman of Fulta.[3]

During the Governor-Generalship of Lord Minto the important Dutch possessions of Moluccas (1810) and Java as well as its dependencies (August, 1811) were captured by the British

1. Nolan, op. cit., p. 491.
2. Henry Douglas served as the Judge-Magistrate of Patna from 1792 till the 6th September, 1810. During the short periods of his temporary absence in the year 1806, Charles Patton, Registrar of the Court of Appeal, Patna, and then Charles F. Sealy, Assistant Judge of the Diwani Adalat of Patna, officiated in his place. Most probably, in recognition of his useful and conscientious services, the Government elevated Douglas to the position of a Judge, and ultimately to that of the first Judge, of the Court of Appeal and Circuit for the Patna Division. In this capacity also he discharged his duties satisfactorily for a number of years. He died at Patna in 1839. His tomb is located in the European cemetry of the mid-nineteenth century, opposite Pirbahore Police Station on the southern side of the main road.
3. Patna District Judge Court Records.

Indian Government.[1] "An Empire", as Auber observes, "which for two centuries had contributed to the power, prosperity and grandeur of one of the principal and most respected states of Europe was wrested from the short usurption of the French Government, added to the dominions of the British Crown, and converted from a seat of hostile machinations and commercial competition, into an augmentation of British power and prosperity"[2]. In October, 1811, Thomas Stamford Bingley Raffles was appointed "provisional" Governor of Java.[3]

The first article of the Convention, concluded between the Governments of Great Britain and the Netherlands on the 13th August, 1814, provided, as has been already noted, for restoration to the latter of all the "colonies, Establishments, which were possessed by Holland after commencement of the late war (i.e., before 1794-95), in the Seas and on the continents of America, Africa and Asia with certain exceptions specified".[4] These exceptions in India were Cochin and Baranagore. F. A. Van Braam was appointed Commissioner at Chinsura to repossess the settlements of the King of Netherlands in India. He deputed Frasis Cassiarees Kegal in 1817 to receive charge of the Dutch establishments at Patna and Dacca. In fact, by the next year the Dutch got back all their Indian possessions with the exceptions noted above.

---

1. Nolan, op. cit., Vol. II, pp. 531-35.
2. Auber, Rise and Progess of the British Power in India, Vol. II, Ch. XII, p. 47.
3. In 1805 Raffles (1781—1826) was appointed Assistant Secretary to the Governor of Penang. He was transferred to Malacea in 1808. He visited Calcutta in 1810 and then got the appointment of Agent to the Governor-General with the Malaya States. On the 4th December, 1810, he started for Malacca to make preparations for the expedition that resulted in the British annexation of Java. He was "provisional" Governor of Java from October, 1811 until 1816. He went to England in March, 1816, published his 'History of Java' in 1817 and was soon knighted. He sailed for the East once again in November, 1817, and reached Bencoolen in March 1818 as Lieutenant Governor. He finally left Bencoolen for England in 1824, and died there on the 5th July, 1826.
4. Appendix Q.

CHAPTER VII

Cession of the Dutch possessions in India to the British Government, 1824-25

Even after the Dutch had got back their settlements in the East, with some exceptions, in 1816-1818, the functionaries of their Government and those of the British Government were engaged in various negotiations on some conflicting questions. Sir Thomas Stamford Bingley Raffles, who went to Bencoolen with the designation of Lieutenant Governor in March, 1818, was "intimately acquainted with the various interests in that quarter, and with the positions which presented the best means for successfully competing with the preponderating influence of the Dutch...."[1]. The hoisting of British flag on Singapore by Sir Stamford Raffles "brought matters to an open issue"[2]. The points in dispute being referred to the English Company's government in Bengal, Marquis of Hastings lavished, in a *Minute*, ample praise on Sir Stamford Raffles for his zeal to uphold British interests and at the same time pressed upon the Home Government the expediency of a speedy settlement with the Dutch[3]. The negotiations between the British Government and the Government of the Netherlands were protracted till the year 1824 as reference had to be made, on various points, to their respective officers in India[4].

It was during the administration of Lord Amherst that the two came to an agreement providing for mutual exchange of settlements in the East. The English thereby obtained some territorial possessions of great value in strengthening the edifice of the British empire in the East. On the 17th March, 1824, a treaty[5] was signed at London between the British Government and the Government of the Netherlands with a view, as they

---

1. Auber, Rise and Progress of the British Power in India, Vol. II, pp. 555—56.
2. Ibid.
3. Ibid.
4. Ibid.
5. Consultations, 3rd February, 1825, No. 2.

declared, "to place upon a footing mutually beneficial to their respective possessions and the commerce of their subjects in the East Indies so that the welfare and prosperity of both Nations may be promoted in all time to come, without those differences and jealousies which have, in former times, interrupted the Harmony which ought always to subsist between them, and being anxious that all occasions of misunderstanding between their respective agents may be, as much as possible, prevented......"[1].

The important terms of the treaty were as follows :—

"Art. 8—His Netherlands Majesty cedes to His Brittanic Majesty all establishments on the continent of India, and renounces all privileges and exemption enjoyed or claimed in virtue of those establishments.

Art. 9 The factory of Fort Marlborough, all the English possessions on the island of Sumatra are hereby ceded to His Netherlands Majesty; and His Brittanic Majesty further engages that no British settlement shall be formed on that island, nor any treaty concluded by the British authority with the native Prince, chief or state therein.

Art. 10—Town and port of Malacca and dependenceies ceded to Brittanic Majesty.

Art. 11—His Brittanic Majesty withdraws objection to the occupation of the Island of Billiton and dependencies by agents of Netherlands Government.

Art. 12—His Netherlands Majesty withdraws objection to the occupation of the Island of Singapore by subjects of His Brittanic Majesty. No British establishment to be made on the Corimon island and island of Baltam, Bintang, or other islands.

Art. 13—Delivery of all possessions on the 1st March, 1825.

Art. 14—Inhabitants for 6 years of the date of notification of the Treaty may dispose of property as they like".

In accordance with articles 8 and 13 of this treaty, Sir Thomas Munro, Governor in Council at Fort St. George, appointed Lieutenant Colonel James Stuart Fraser, special Agent for foreign settlements, to be Commissioner for receiving possession

1. Proceedings, Foreign Department, 14th October, 1824.

of all such Netherlands Establishments as were within the territories subject to the Governments of Fort St. George from such person or persons as would be duly empowered by the Netherlands Government to deliver up the same[1]. The appointment of Lieutenant Colonal Fraser, and the power as well as insturctions given to him by the Madras Government, were approved of by the Governor-General in Council early in February, 1825[2].

Instructions had been already issued, on the 13th January, 1825, to the Magistrates and the Collectors of Hugli, Murshidabad, Dacca, Patna, Cuttack, and the Twentyfour Parganas appointing them Commissioners to take charge respectively of '*The Town and Territory of Chinsura*', and the Dutch factories and possessions at Kalikapur (near Kassimbazar in the Murshidabad District), at Dacca, at Patna, at Balasore and at Fultah[3].

On the 7th May, 1825, Chinsura was formally delivered by B. C. D. Bouman, Commissioner appointed on behalf of the Netherlands Government, to W. H. Belli and D. C. Smyth, Commissioners on behelf of the British Government[4]. The total sum transferred by the former to the latter was Sicca Rupees 57,735-6-10½.[5] They deposited the cash together with the promissory notes and Bills of Exchange in the treasury of the Collector of the Hugli District awaiting the orders of their Government on the subject[6], and took possession of some arms, ammunition, papers and documents.

The British Commissioners made some important observations, for the knowledge of their Government, in their letter to C. Lushington, Secretary to Government, Fort William, dated the 7th May, 1825 :—"The Netherlands Commissioner wished to enter into some discussion regarding the Chinsurah

---

1. Proceedings, Foreign Department. 3rd February, 1325, No. 2.
2. Letter from C. Lushington, Secretary to Govt., Fort William, to D. Hill, Secretary to Government, Fort St. George, 1825.
3. Proceedings, Foreign Department, 13th January, 1825, No. 15.
4. Letter from Commissioners for receiving charge of Chinsura to C. Lushington, Secretary to Government, Fort William, dated 7th May, 1825; Proceedings, Foreign Department, dated 19th May, 1825, No. 7.
5. Proceedings, Foreign Dept., 19th May, 1825, No. 7.
6. Ibid

appeals, now depending before the Supreme Court at Batavia, as well as the cases of those individuals who might under the existing Dutch Law be still entitled to an appeal. We however informed the Commissioner, that being solely commissioned to receive charge of the settlement we did not consider ourselves authorized to enter into any discussion on this point, but that the Netherlands authorities might rest assured, that any question of the sort that might eventually arise, would be duly considered by the British Government in the proper Department, and would certainly receive a fair and liberal construction.

The Commissioner also alluded to the cases of certain individuals, who had taken refuge in Chinsura on account of the entanglement of their affairs, and handed us for consideration two petitions from these persons, requesting permission still to reside in Chinsura and not to be liable to the process of the Supreme Court.

On this, as on the former question, we stated that we had no authority either to grant or to reject the prayers of the Petitioners. Being however of opinion that such a request was on general principles utterly inadmissible, we considered it our duty to inform the Commissioner that until we were instructed to the contrary we should conceive oursleves bound to grant every assistance to any offices of the Supreme Court, that should demand it, and we finally suggested, that all persons placed in this unpleasant situation should be informed of our determination, in order to their withdrawing from the Settlement, previous to its formal delivery to the British Commissioners.

The above remarks are all that at present appear necessary to report to Government. The Lists of the Records and of the other official Papers, being all in the Dutch Language, we have made arrangments for their early translation into English, that we may be prepared hereafter to deliver them over to the proper offices, to which they might finally be assigned. The European Dutch Records apparently go back as far as A. D. 1700 and the Persian Furmans (firmans) etc. to 1638 A. D. Amongst the latter documents, appear to be some very curious and authentic papers, which ought we think to be made over to the Presidency Committee of Records, as they may on examination prove to be of some value, and at any rate certainly deserve to be carefully preserved on account of their very great antiquity. The European Records may perhaps be transferred to the Foreign General Departments.

The Police Establishments have been retained by us on their present footing until some arrangements shall have been made by Government in the proper Department. The expense of this Establishment, as well as the expense of translating the Lists of the Records, and any other petty expenses that have been or may be indispensably necessary will be submitted to you at the end of the month, for the purpose of obtaining the authority of Government for their payment.

We beg leave in conclusion to state, that until we receive the further orders of Government, Mr. Belli will conduct the necessary details of this Settlement in the Revenue Department and Mr. Smyth those relating to the Police, and should any question of moment arise, we shall either consult jointly on the subject or submit the case to Government on the occasion as may appear to demand"[1].

They addressed another letter to C. Lushington on the 11th May, 1825, forwarding to him at the same time the following letter, dated the 6th May, 1825, received by them from the Dutch Commissioner, Bouman. The Dutch Commissioner had written therein : "Agreeably to the Instructions wherewith I am furnished, I have the honour to acquaint you, that since the restoration of this place to the Commissioner the late I. A. Van Braam Esqr in 1817 several plaints have been preferred to His Excellency the Governor General in Council at Batavia by persons who felt aggrieved by the decisions of the Netherland Authorities at this place, but whereas in so doing the necessary formalities were not observed, no enquiry or investigation, into the nature of such plaints had ever been entered into. And although the time given for appeals by your Regulations should have expired, I have it in command to state, that His Excellency the Governor General in Council at Batavia aforesaid is desirous that to such persons access may be granted to British Authorities for redress, and that thereof public notice be given I have to request you will have the goodness to submit this case to the

1. Ibid.

Right Hon'ble the Governor General in Council at Fort William and trust it will meet with very liberal consideration"[1].

In acknowledging the receipt of the letters of the English Commissioners at Chinsura, dated the 7th and 11th May, 1825, C. Lushington informed them on the 19th May, 1825, that with regard to the several important questions they had represented therein for the consideration of their Government in Calcutta, the Governor-General in Council deemed it advisable "to suspend a decision on them" until they had been able by continuing to "act in conjoint capacity of Commissioners," to "furnish a more detailed report of the various points arising out of the transfer" together with their opinions and suggestions on each head of reference[2]. He, however, communicated to them that their proceedings, as described in these letters, were "generally approved"[3] of by the Governor-General and Council. On the same day a notice was published in the Government Gazette regarding the formal delivery of 'the Town and Settlement of Chinsura' by the Netherlands Government to the British Government on the 7th May, 1825[4].

The Dutch factory at Kalikapur had not yet been delivered to the English Commissoners there, Travers and Magniac, who brought it to the notice of the Calcutta Government on the 11th May 1825[5]. C. Lushington, therefore, instructed the English Commissioners at Chinsura on the 19th May next to apply to Bouman "to expedite the transfer of Calcapore" (Kalikapur) and inform Travers and Magniac of the result of their application[6]. Most probably, the matter was quickly settled.

---

1. Ibid.
2. Ibid.
3. Ibid.
4. Ibid.
5. Ibid.
6. Ibid.

Appendix A

"In consequence of a Contract entered into by Monsr. Drabbe, Chief, on the part of the Dutch Company at Patna, to make over to us our share of all the Saltpetre which he has bought or may buy during the course of this year at the rate of Sa. Rs. 3-4 per maund of *Dobara,* as it is specified in the Contract signed by the said Gentleman, We the French and English Chiefs at Patna have agreed to the following Articles, Viz.

Article 1st.

Mr. Drabbe shall acquaint us when and where he will have the Saltpetre ready to deliver, that we may send people to receive it, paying the charges of transportation.

2nd.

Every bag of Saltpetre shall weigh 145 Dutch Pounds as is customary at the above mentioned price Rs. 3 As. 4 per maund and the Bag must hold two maunds.

3rd.

The *Batta*[1] of the Rupees which we may pay shall be at the rate of $6\frac{1}{2}$ per cent and Mr. Drabbe or his Agent must give receipts for the sums paid.

4th.

The Duty called *Iragique* which must be paid being Sa Rs. 3100 shall be charged as usual, Viz.

By the french Sa Rs.	465	
By the English..	1317-8-	Sa Rs.
By the Dutch ..	1317-8-	3100

5th.

We have agreed that Mr. Drabbe alone shall buy up all the Saltpetre, and cause our share to be delivered to us as soon as possible that we may be enabled to dispatch our Ship in September next.

---

1. Vide Glossary.

6th.

Whoever may be charged with the purchase of Saltpetre for the following year, shall be obliged to furnish the Chiefs of the other two nations with their share as Mr. Drabbe has bound himself to do this year.

7th.

In case of any Merchants owing Mr. Drabbe money, the person who may be charged with the purchase of Saltpetre for the next year shall not buy any from those who are so indebted unless they previously settle their Accounts with the said Gentleman.

8th.

The English shall have a third of the Saltpetre which is collected at Moon and the Dutch the rest provided they pay 15 per cent to the French.

9th.

The Saltpetre which is collected at Chappra, Jaunagor, Derferry, Singulia, Mongor, Monia Telipour, Mennipore, Beaguinpour, shall be divided as follows,

To the French — 15 —
— the English — 42 — ½
— — -- Dutch 42 — ½

100 — being 15 per cent for the French and the rest to be equally divided between the English and the Dutch.

10th.

Mr. Drabbe shall pay the Duty of brokerage to our brokers, as likewise the person who may be charged with the purchase of Saltpetre next year.

11th.

In case Government causes any hindrance to Mr. Drabbe in the purchase of Saltpetre, we will jointly complain, but without being obliged to be at any of the cost, which Mr. Drabbe may be forced to make on this affair.

12th.

If any of the Merchants refuse to sell their Saltpetre this year.

the person who may be charged with the purchase next year shall not buy any of that Saltpetre at above 3 Rs. the maund, but under it if he can.

13th.

Agreeable to the abovementioned Articles we promise Mr. Drabbe to buy no Saltpetre this year nor to suffer our Agent to buy any, & to send to Mr. Drabbe all the Merchants of the Territory of Patna who may address themselves to us, that they may contract with him.

Copy of the Treaty entered into between the Chiefs of the three European Nations at Patna relative to the Trade of Saltpetre.

Sign'd/- Jos Briggs
Secretary

I, the underwritten do hereby promise to furnish the French & English with their contingency of all the Saltpetre of Obara (Dobara) which is refined, which I have contracted for & may

r. a.
contract to the end of December 1744 at 3 4 Sicca, excepting what may remain in the Factory & of which I shall declare the true quantity, on condition that these Gentlemen act in the same manner towards me next year, to which they shall engage themselves in writing, likewise that neither they nor their Agents shall buy Saltpetre at any place or under any pretext whatsover, nor shall they receive any into their Factories or other places dependant on them, that the purchase shall be made by me along as likewise by whoever may be charged with the remainder next year, that we may bring over the Merchants to reasonable Terms and to avoid paying an excessive a great loss to the Chiefs. For the abovementioned reasons and for the common interests of the three Nations, we have resolved to carry it on in conjuction, experience having taught us that this Trade when carried on separately has been the means of increasing the price of great losses & bad debts, by the Nations raising it thro' emulation with one another.

I promise to fulfill the abovementioned articles, which are to remain in full force. But if I am informed that the English or French or both have committed any breach of this contract which they have charged me with, it is then to be considered as invalid.

Having signed two copies of this Treaty of the same tenor one being accomplished the other to be void. One of them is in possession of Mr. Gillander and the other in that of Mr. Barwell.

In the Dutch Factory the 28th March 1744.

A true Copy

Signed/- Benton de Louson"

Appendix B

We the underwritten Chiefs on the part of the French, English & Dutch Companys, do hold as good & valid the Contract entered into the 8th Jany last respecting the purchase of Saltpetre, by our Superiors in Bengal, & also any alterations which time & occasion may require. For Present year we have entrusted Mr. Drabble Chief for the Dutch Compy. with the purchase of all the Saltpetre to made who alone is to have charge of it.

Article 1.

No Alteration shall be made in the present Contract by us or by our Successors without the approbation of our Superiors in Bengal.

2nd.

The Chief for the part of the Dutch is alone to purchase the Saltpetre as is above specified, & shall be obliged to furnish the other two Nations, the maund weighing 72½ lb Dutch lb at the rate of 3¼ Rs. Sea. & to deliver at the abovementioned places.

3rd.

We the French & English Chiefs do promise, to make no advances nor to contract with any Merchants for Saltpetre but to refer them to the Dutch Chief.

4th.

The Division of the Saltpetre is to be as follows.

On every 100 Mds. the French to have 15 Mds.
the English — — — — — — — — — — — — — — 42 ½
the Dutch — — — — — — — — — — — — — — 42 ½

Excepting what is collected at *Man*, the French shall have 15 P. Ct But as the English never contracted for any great quantity in this place before they shall only have a third of the produce of man.

5th.

The Saltpetre to be delivered at the undermentioned place, viz., Chapra, Singia man Monnipour Sundy Fatipour Derfary

Bekenpour & Moneer.

6th.

Each Nation to cause it then to be weighed & transported at its own expenee.

7th.

If any Saltpetre is reced. by our former Debtors after the signing of this contract we promise to divide it as above specified making good the difference to the furnisher.

8th.

After the signing of this contract we shall each of us declare the just quantity of Saltpetre which remains in our respective Factories which we may keep without making any subdivisions.

We shall as is usual pay to the Government of the *Attruphy* amounting to 3500 Rs. Sa. in the following manner viz.

The French — — — — — — — — — — — — — —	Sa Rs.	500
The English — — — — — — — — — — — — — —		1500
The Dutch — — — — — — — — — — — — — —		1500

10th.

We shall lend our Couldrons & ca. to whomsoever Mr. Drabbe pleases.

11th.

After signing this present contract, we the French & English Chiefs promise to make use of no violence or otherwise to the people whom Mr. Drabbe may appoint to purchase the Saltpetre.

12th.

We will receive the Saltpetre when Mr. Drabbe acquaint us it is proper to do so.

13th.

We are to take up the Saltpetre 3 days after Mr. Drabbe has made us acquainted of its being ready, as whatever accidents that may happen to it after that period is to be at our own loss & not that of Mr. Drabbe.

14th.

When the Saltpetre is ready Mr. Drabbe is to give each nation its just proportion, without one's being either preferred or receiving its share before the other.

15th.

We promise likewise to Mr. Drabbe, that in case of his meeting with any impediment in the purchase of Saltpetre either from the Government at Patna or from any of the Fouzdars[1] Jemidars[2] & others jointly to oppose them, each Nation being at an equal proportion of the expences incurred.

16th.

We shall each of us furnish our Share of the Saltpetre which it may require for the making of powder or any thing.

17th.

We promise to furnish Mr. Drabbe with what money he may have occasion for in the purchase of Saltpetre according to our respective proportions, experience having shew'd us that it is necessary to make advances for that.

18th.

We likewise promise Mr. Drabbe to bear an equal proportion of the losses he may meet with in the delivery of Saltpetre or for the sums of money which may remain in the hands of the merchants & which it is almost impossible to recover. Mr. Drabbe being obliged to furnish us with an exact acct. of the said money.

Not a Seer of Saltpetre is to be bought of Displond (Deepchand) or of any of the merchants, until they have toward their price to the same as the merchants. We have contracted with, but if they refuse to do it, we shall take more from them that they may not give laws to the Nations.

19th.

In case Displond (Deepchand) or any of the merchants transport their Saltpetre to Bengal Our Superiors of Chandernagore Calcutta Chinsurah shall do every thing in their power to hinder their disposing of it.

---

1. Faujdars.
2. Zamindars.

We the undersigned do hold as good & valid this contract of which we have made 3 copies in each Language which we have approved & signed for the approbation of our Superiors in Bengal.

Patna 26 April 1746
Signed/-Guillander
Will : Barwell
Drabbe."

Appendix C

Translation of a copy of a Perwannah under the Seal of the Nabob. Metteemen ul Mulk Sujah ul Dowlah Sujah ul Dien Mahomed Cawn Bahader Assed Jung, dated the 21st of Zehedge in the 11th Year of his present Majesty's reign.

"To All Muhuddees (?), and those who are entrusted with affairs of Government. To all Fougidars[1], Carories[2] Jagheerdara[3] and Zemindars for the present and future of the Subah of Bengal and Orissa, Be it known that in the Imperial Mandates issued during the administration of the deceased Emperor, and in different Perwannahs[4] which have been granted by the Nazims, and Dewans, it is ordered that the Agents of the General on the part of the Dutch Company shall bring their Ships to the ports of Houghly; Balasore, and Pipley and Anchor them at whatever place they please : that they shall pay the established Duties of $2\frac{1}{2}$ Rupees at one place only, at the Port of Houghly that after paying Duties on their Merchandize they shall carry it to be disposed of wherever they please; that they shall purchase of whatever Merchants they please, employ in their Business, whatever Delolls[5] they please make purchases in the provinces at whatever place they please, and dispatch their goods to the said Ports; that no person shall impede or obstruct them for Rhadarry[6] Duties : press their Boats, or commit other acts, which have been prohibited at the Imperial Court: That when they have brought their Ships to the aforementioned ports, neither their own private nor hired Boats shall be seized for Kattabarra[7]: that they shall keep

Guard as usual that no demand of duties shall be made at Murbatry (?), upon Wheat or Rice which they may purchase

1. Faujdars.
2. Croris.
3. Jagirdars.
4. Parwanahs.
5. Vide Glossary.
6. Ibid.
7. Ibid.

for their own consumption; that no demands of duties upon their Goods and merchandize shall be repeated that the Village of Chinsurah in the Purgannah of Kasbah (?) and Barnargur in the Purgannah of Calcutta, Bazar, Mirzapore, dependent on the Bukshbunder[1], have long been under the administration of the Dutch Company : that in order to fit up their Ships they shall employ Carpenters, Smiths, and other Artificers and Labourers to inhabit these places and the Rents of the said Village shall annually be received according to the established Jumma[2], without being subject to any increassed demands or liable to any seizure or Imposition of Conna, Somarrah or otherwise. These shall be remitted—should any of their own servants, Baparries[3] or Pykars[4] be guilty of smuggling any of their own Goods on Board the Dutch Vessels besides the Goods belonging to the Dutch Company, and shall be detected and taken up for such a practice by their Fiscal; the Mutsuddies[5] and Officers of the Government are not to interfere, or take part with such persons, nor are they to suffer any person to buy such Goods without the knowledge of the Dutch : that upon the Gold, Silver and Copper which the Dutch may dispatch from the Port of Hougly to Moorshedabad Jehanguernagur[6], Akbernagur[7] &ca the Derogha[8] or officers of the mints are to receive the Duty which have been long established of $2\frac{1}{2}$ Rupees and first to coin into sicca the Bullion of the Dutch, that they may be encouraged, and may dispatch their Ships in due Season—It is therefore written that you conform to the Sacred Firmaun[9] as infallible as Fate, and to the Different Sunnuds[10] which have been granted from Nazims & Dewans to Jacob Sadeland Director and agent of the General on the part of the Dutch Company, in order

---

1. Ibid.
2. Ibid.
3. Ibid.
4. Ibid.
5. Ibid.
6. Dacca.
7. Rajmahal.
8. Daroga—An Overseer or Superintendent.
9. Firman.
10. Sanads.

that the Dutch may without molestation attend to the management of their Affairs, and be encouraged to increase their Trade more than before—On this occasion know the strictest Injunctions : do not deviate from nor call for fresh Sunnuds every year."

Appendix D

A Perwannah from the Nabob Mohubut Jung (Mahabat Jang Alivardi Khan) dated the 19th Mohurram in the 29th year of the Glorious Reign.

"To the Mutsuddies of the Buxbunder, Present and Future of the Subah of Bengal, be it known."

"The Vakeel[1] of the Dutch Company hath represented that there is Collected on the Goods of the Dutch Company a duty of 2½ Pr. Cent and on the Goods of Private Merchants 3½ Pr. Cent, by reason of which many of the Private Dutch Merchants have desisted from carrying on Trade and consequently great loss arises to the Sahir[2] of the Buxbunder. If the Duty of Private Merchants is fixed at the same rate[3], with that of the Company, there will be a considerable increase in the Trade of this Country, and it will even exceed the Trade of former times from which great advantage will arise in the duties.

"For this reason be it known that it is resolved the Private Dutch Merchants shall carry on Trade in the same manner as the Company and shall pay the same Duties, and be it further known that as you are to Collect the same duties from them as from the Company so shall you collect same abwab[4].

(Secret Consultations, 11 November, 1776, No. X.)

---

1. Vakil.
2. Sayer.
3. See ante.
4. Abwab "Miscellaneous cesses, imports and charges levied in addition to the regular assessment or the land".

Appendix E

Treaty between the Dutch East India Company and the Nawab of Bengal, For. Cons 25 Aug. 1760.

Articles Agreed on by the undermentioned Deputies appointed by the Directors and Council for the Dutch East India Company in Bengal to be performed on the part of the said Company and conditions granted them in consequence by the Nabob Jaffer Ally Cawn, Sujah-Al Moulk Behadre, Mahaubut Jung the performance of which said Articles and conditions are at the request of both the contracting parties guaranteed to them respectively by the undersigned and Council of Fort William.

Article 1st.

The Directors and Council shall immediately send away from Chinchura and their other Factories all the Europeans they have exceeding the number of One hundred and twenty five granted them by Treaty; The said men may remain on Board of their Ships at Culpee or Fulta till an opportunity offers of conveying them to Batavia.

2nd.

That if they have erected any new Fortifications or deepen'd or Widen'd their Ditch since the execution of their Treaty with the Nabob they shall be immediateley reduced to their former condition.

3rd.

That if they have augmented their number of Guns or their quantitary of Military stores beyond what is necessary for the ordinary uses of their Factory the overplus shall immediately be sent away in the same manner as is mentioned in the first article regarding the men.

4th.

That they shall never suffer more than one Europe Ship at a time to come higher up the River than Culpee, Fulta or Myapore without the express leave of the Nabob first obtained.

5th.

The said Deputies on the part of the said Directors and Council do hereby renew, confirm and ratify all the conditions by them agreed on in the Treaty concluded between the English Commissiaries on behalf of the Nabob and the Commissaries on the part of the said Directore and Council the 3rd of December 1759 and more expressly and particularly that part which limit their forces in Bengal to the number of one hundred and twenty five Europeans.

6th.

The said Directore and Council shall now and at all times when the Nabob may require it permit an Officer of his together with an English Officer to review the men and military stores in Chinchura and their other factories. Or if any other means can be agreed on between the Governor and Council of Fort William and the Directore and Council of Chinchura whereby the number of the men and the quantity of Military stores may be ascertained to the satisfaction of the said Governor and Council of Fort William so as that they may be enabled to answer to the Nabob as Guarantees for the security of his country. In such case the Nabob will not insist upon the review.

7th.

The Nabob's Duan Ray Rayen Ameed Ray on the behalf of the Nabob solemnly engages to the said Directore and Council that on their complying with the before going conditions they shall hereafter be supported in all their Rights, Liberties and Prerogatives in Trade as granted them by the Phirmaunds of the Mogul.

8th.

That they shall in future be burthen'd with no new or unusual Taxes or Contributions whatsoever—and particularly they shall be free from the payment of the sum enacted from them for some years past by the Subah of Patna under the title of Peshcush due for the previlege of the trade of Saltpeter; it not being just that the said Directore and Council should continue to pay for a privilege that they do not now hold.

9th.

That they shall have a free and uninterrupted passage for their ships and vessels on the River with the exception mentioned in the 4th Article as also for their Oxen, Carts, Cooleys, Peons, Cossids[1] & ca, by land to their usual destin'd Place with the seal of the Company and that of the Directore or Chiefs on other servants properly qualified without being subject to any impositions from any Phousdars, Jageerdars, Chowkeydars, Droghers or other officers of the Government.

10th.

That in consequence of the several Phirmaunds by them obtained, The Dutch East India Company's Trade in the Provinces of Bengal, Bihar and Orisa shall be free and uninterrupted in all articles whatsover, excepting the purchase of Saltpetre of which the Nabob has granted to the English, the Exclusive Priviledge.

11th

That the Nabob will order the account of their coinage in the Mint at Cariemabaad to be adjusted and the balance which may appear due to be discharged and that in future their Business in the said Mint shall be carried on without Molestation or hindrance, and the nett produce be delivered without any detention or unlawfull deduction.

Done at Fort William this 23rd of August 1760.

The above mentioned Articles having been duly ratified by the Nabob on one part and on the other by the Directore and Council of Chinchura, are now signed by us the Governor and

1. Messengers.

Council of Fort William as Guarantees.

Done at Fort William this 22nd day of September 1760.

Signed/—Henry Vansittart
John Caillaud
Wm. B. Sumner
T. T. Holwell
W. Mc. Gwuire
S. S. Verelst
S. L. Smyth
Culling Smith."

Appendix F

Sec. Cons. 10 Feby 1774 No. 4.

"To Mr. Warren Hastings

Governor on the part of the Hon'ble English Company.

Sir,

Mr. Falk has made a Report to the Council of the Conference held with you, relative to the Peishcush, He has at the same time communicated to us the Reasons which you were pleased to alledge for its continuation, as well as his refutation; Give me leave Sir, to represent to you with respect to the Affair in Question that the Maxim which establishes a Rule that the present Government should Enjoy the same advantages with the former can be valid only when founded upon just and lawful Claims. The Peishcush[1] Tribute was never allowed or acknowledged as such by us : we never submitted to it, but the Law of the most Powerful, obliged us against our Inclination, to satisfy the arbitrary claims of Regents of the Country. Be kind enough, Sir, to consider how far it is becoming to undertake to justify an Act of Violence, or to make a Law of it; and Whether the present Government, is under the absolute necessity of following, in this affair, the example of the preceding one.

In order to be made fully sensible of the Illegality of the Peishcush, we need only look into its origin, of which I have given you. Sir, a detail in my foregoing; and I was persuaded you would consider the affair in the same light, after having been made so fully acquainted with all its circumstances, which as I have reason to think you are.

On this account Sir, I cannot help being very much astonished to find that so manifest and open an attack upon our Privileges and Liberty's, and which is so directly opposite to the Tenor of our Firmauns, should at this Time, be considered in the light of a Claim, justified and authorized, by a long course of years, in

1. "A tribute, quit rent or a present, paid to Government, as an acknowledgement for any tenure, etc."

such manner as to become of equal validity with an antient right, and the Reason given that it is a possession acknowledged and allowed on the one hand, & an involuntary submission on the other. Such arguments however as these fall to the Ground as soon as made use of, for be so good, Sir, as to consider what species of Right a Claimant, adjudging to himself the possession of a thing can invest him with Nobody would surely speak up to their own Prejudice, but it is nevertheless certain that could we agree with you as to the Justice of the Claim, it would be Means of adding a very considerable Degree of weight to it. A disinterested judge who would declare the pretention to be well grounded would at once put an end to the Dispute, but this not being the case, the Acquiescence of one of the Parties concerned can never be substituted in its Room, Besides, Sir, we never submitted to this act of Violence but when forcibly obliged to it : for not a year has passed that our Trade has not met with all manner of Obstacles. Our Boats on the River have been stopped, the People in our Service have been most unmercifully treated, and many other excesses been committed to lay us under the necessity of paying this Tribute. If then we must tamely submit to see ourselves ill used, having no power to screen ourselves by resisting such treatment you will yourself, Sir easily agree with us that such a Species of submission can never serve to justify the Usurper.

I have had the honor, Sir, to inform you of the Reasons which occasioned the Free Gift made from Motives of Gratitude to the Subahdar of Patna. It was for protecting our Mercantile Fleets with his Troops against the Insults of other Vagabonds. But this Gift which proceeded from gratitude, cannot in any manner serve to establish the Claim of the Peishcush. It was by no means reasonable to require from us an acknowledgment, as soon as that Protection was at an End it was no longer necessary. In spite of all this the Regents of the Country who formerly protected us from Foreign Insults, have gone over to the opposite extreme, by becoming themselves our Tyrants, they have demanded and got from us by Force, by way of Tribute, a Gift which we had been accustomed to make them in return for the services which they had rendered us, and they have from Time to Time raised the Value of this sum to seven times its original Amount.

As our Free Gifts, Sir, made in former Times cannot therefore be alleged in support of the Peishcush which was forcibly taken from us by tyrannical Power, never having been acknowleged by us as either just or lawful, and which we never paid but when obliged to it by Force—The Council, Sir, cannot agree to your proposal nor consent to 15,000 Rupees to Government, and 5000 to the Dewan at Patna since by a like Composition a Claim which we now Dispute with you on good Grounds would become an incontrovertable Right, of which we never so much as entertained the least Idea. On the contrary Sir, the Council beg you will be kind enough to bestow a more ample consideration on the Representations which I have just now made to you, as well as to those which I formely laid before you, and that made to you by our Agent at Patna, and hope, that you will be pleased to employ your kind assistance for the entire abolition of the Peishcush.

I have the honor to be
Sir &ca &ca
Sd/-Bacheracht"

Appendix G

"Memorial treating of the State of the Dutch East India Company with Respect to their Trade in General in the Kingdoms of Bengal Bahar & Orixa their Rights & privileges; commencing from the year 1756 till this date and the necessity together with the Means of Re-establishing them presented & laid before the Hon'ble Warren Hastings Governor General & the Gentlemen of the Council at Calcutta, composing the Supreme Board of Government in Bengal &ca on behalf of the Hon'ble English East India Company; by the undersigned Director & Councillors on behalf of the abovementioned Dutch East India Company.

It will be needless for us to enter into a Detail of the General Calamity which for a series of these twenty years past have befallen this rich Country, which we inhabit, and of the universal Decline of its commerce, & finances, which are the Sinews of a well regulated State, and much more so, to set forth the Reasons & causes that have reduced the affairs to so deplorable a situation; The Politicks of your own Nation have so clearly been productive of them, and you yourselves are so fully convinced thereof, that we should give ourselves a superfluous trouble to do it. We persuade ourselves also, that a geneal Reformation was the Chief object in view, in the arrangement made by the British Government, and that you were directed thereby, to make the attainment of it in the best manner possible the Chief End of your Deliberations.

But the Chain of misfortune and Disgraces, with which the Dutch Company during all that period to the present Instant the Dutch Company has had to struggle within their Trade; the Indignity and outrages which they and their Dependants have suffered upon many occasions; in fine the affront and violence offered, to them, have been as well the particular objects of our Resentment as the Motives and cause of our Constant Complaints. We flatter ourselves however that these having been carried to extremity are at length 'brought to that period in which we may hope for amendment, we expect it Gentlemen from your Justice and Equity, and in that reliance we take the Liberty to lay before you in this Memorial, our situation and our Grievances.

To which End it appears sufficient for us to confine ourselves to a demonstration.

1stly.

Of the Rights and Privileges which the Dutch Company have obtained in the Country at an immense expense, of the several Firmaunds from the Sovereigns of these Kingdoms and their Representatives, more than once received, confirmed and extended.

2ndly.

Of the Infringemets that have been made upon them from Time to Time and particularly within the last Eighteen years.

3rdly.

That we now mean to claim from you at this Junction, the Putting them upon their former footing since the English Company has declared itself Dewan or Representative of the Sovereign.

With respect to the first point, The trade of the Dutch Company, is from its infancy and first commencement, in Bengal and Surat, taken notice of in the Firmaunds of the respective Emperors of Indostan astonding to the Improvement of the Country and Increase of the Revenues. They therefore obtained by the Firmaunds the power and Liberty of carrying on a free and unmolested Trade throughout this Kingdom, in whatever Places their Dependants might land, without let, Hindrance or Molestation from any person whomsoever, much less to be Subject to Extortions and Affronts Under the General Head of all produces, are in particular comprehended, Linnens, Silk, Silk-Stuffs, Ophium Salt-petre and Borax, as likewise the purchase of Grain. These privileges are successively received in some of the Firmaunds extended. The Right to the Coinage of and Silver, and the payment of $2\frac{1}{2}$ pct. for import Export Duties once in the year at fixed Places, is also included therein. Unlimited jurisdiction over the Company's Servants and the Right of exercising justice in Civil cases and of inflicting such punishment in criminal ones as do not reach to Capital, upon the other inhabitants of their colonies, being considered their subject and claim their Right. The Detention of their Ships and other vessels by which the course of affairs may be impeded, is thereby strictly forbidden in a word the Company has obtained these Firmaunds, so particular and extensive a right and power, nothing but open violence can overthrow or destroy the same.

What numberless instances might we produce of the oppression what we have been obliged to submit to, and what a catalogue of complaints would it not form, if, in order to prove, according to our second position, the infringement which our aforeseaid privileges have undergone, we were to speak of every particular act of Injustice, that has been done us. In vain have we ever endeavoured, by prudence and conduct to avoid and prevent those misfortunes, or not succeeding therein to obtain by Complaints and Remonstrances, a proper Redress for the infringements on our Rights and Privileges. These are however of so much weight and authority that all that has been advanced, said or done against them, can bear only the appellation of an open contempt for the most incontestable Right, and a most shamefull oppression.

That our Rights and Privileges may nevertheless not be brought in doubt, or be thought of less extent, than we mention, we request that we may send you such attested copies of our Firmaunds and other Grounds as you may require, or that we may shew the originals to such persons as you may judge proper to depute hither, that are versed in the Persian Language and worthy of your confidence.

We must further beg leave to observe to you Gentlemen, that the Trade of the Dutch Company has exclusive of a few Cavils and disputes which have disappeared from Time to Time, with covetous and unust Princes, which seldom lasted long always been carried on without interruption moreover that an unlimited freedom of Trade was granted to the other Privileged natives equally with general means as they could always enjoy to their full Desire; but that this has met with a considerable check since the famous Revolution of the year 1756.

From that time, or more properly after the taking of Calcutta, and the repeated Victories obtained in the year 1757, over the Soubahs of the Country, the vexation and Calamities increased. We were molested in every Branch of Commerce and our several investments decreased yearly. The right of purchasing Saltpetrefirst Hand, was put a stop to, by the Exclusive privilege, which Lord Clive had taken care to obtain on behalf of the English Company in this Article. The Ophium, an article of so such importance, that was also endeavoured to be wrested from us by numberless Chicanerys and by the Pernicous monopolies of individuals; and the little we were able to obtain thereof, as it were by a sufferance, we were obliged to pay at the highest Rate without being able to this very hour to obtain by near so much as is yearly necessary to complete our usual Demands. The same Evil, namely the in-discrimnate investment of unprivileged Traders and the regulated means of constraint brought into practice, have not only occassioned a general decline in the produces of the Country, but are also the cause, that cloths, silk stuffs, are decreased in quantity and quality, and nevertheless risen to a most exorbitant Price; in so much that, shortly before these Events, we were able to provide cargoes for 12 or 13 ships whereas by the Decrease from year to year it is with the greatest difficulty that we are now able to dispatch loaded in but time, two ships for Europe and but one for India.

All this is so Evident & Well known to the world, that it requires no particular Proof : a comparison of what is now paid by us into the Treasury of this Government with what used to be in the flourishing Days, will forcibly evince the Truth thereof. We need not therefore enlarge upon the subject, only meaning to speak briefly of the principal cause of our complaints in regard to fatal Decline of our Trade.

Since the year 1758 we have from year to year sufficiently had reason to lament the unjust dealing and oppressions of the English Chiefs of the Sub-ordinate Factories, and the Residents and Gomashtas[1] in the accruing. We have shewn and proved that these Disasters put it absolutely out of the power of our Merchants and Gomastas to fulfill their contracts and Engagements with us. There would be no end to the Recital, if we

1. "An Indian Commissioner, factor or agent." Also "a clerk for vernacular correspondence."

repeated here afresh the Particulars of each Circumstance How many Commissions have there not been set on Foot, to enquire into the complaints and we cannot think but that your Honors, or at least the Hon'ble the Governor General Mr. Hastings, are sensible of little success that attended the joint Regulations which were agreed upon in the years 1764 & 1768, to remove for once if Possible the Hindrance which continually prevailed ? How many Times, since the above Period have we not complained of the rash and indiscreet practice of individuals in laying in their investments, when having made themselves masters of an immense quantity, at a Price (it matters not what), ill-treated the weavers, Workers, labourers, and laid them under Engagements not to be performed, in order to satisfy their avarice and Covetousness.

In the meantime the consequences hereof have been, the total destruction of the Cloth-Trade, the enormous Enhancement of every article, the desertion of the Farmers and Manufacturers, and the cause of the considerable Bankrupticies & Arrears among the Weavers; And Prudence, in order to reform their Evil; Whilst it should have invited and encouraged the natives by timely and spirited dealings, to return to their deserted quarters and exercise their Trade & Callings freely, without Interruption or constraint.

We must therefore Gentlemen for the General Good and for the re-establishment of our drooping state, urge you to take these matters most seriously into consideration. We have and are willing to persuade ourselves that you yourselves are convinced of the necessity of so doing, and to lay the Trade open and free from all Restraint, incumbrance and Oppression. The Measures which have been taken for that purpose since the Commencement of Mr. Hastings' Government plainly shew it. But how little to the purpose and how insufficient these Measures have proved hitherto, requires but very little demonstration. Not to speak now of what happened in Patna in the year 1761, 62 & 63 in regard to Ophium, we beg leave to recommend to your attention the Circumstances relative to the cloth Investment at the same place, in the year 1772, when the strictest orders had already been given for Liberty of Trade therein, and that in spite thereof, an insufficient Pyh'ar (Pykar) daringly arrogated to himself the power of openly ill-treating the Weavers and other Artificers that had engaged themselves to the Dutch Company, and to take away from them the goods, for which money had been advanced them for account of our Company. In Dacca there has been introduced a mode inconsistent to every former usage and Custom, and runious to every one that has not in his power, to carry on his Trade by Restraint & Authority; our affairs which are of no considerable Extent were by this mode reduced to the most deplorable condition, and the Abandoning of Dacca is the final Result of all the Vexations, Hindrances and Difficulties with which we have had to struggle and to which we must ascribe the loss of about 20000 rupees which we shall not be able to recover from the Delols, who complain that the means of repairing their losses are entirely taken away from them, by the aforesaid arrangement. What Benefit has resulted from the late published Freedom of Trade in the Aurgungs, dependent upon the Principal Factories ? Have not we since experienced circumstances which give us the greatest Reason for heavy complaints ? Witness what happened in the year 1774 at Mahanendpore[1] and at Buddaul[2]. It is true that since we complained thereof, nothing further has been heard of the kind. But Gentlemen, we believe that we shall remain exposed to one or other inconvenience in case the published Freedom leaves with your European Servants and inland Dependents, the power of judging that Pre-advances made for Account of the Hon'ble English Company, Give a Right of obliging the Weavers in general to fulfill in preference to all others, the Engagements which they may come under with the English Company or others of their Dependants; for not to say, that these Engagements may be extended, without limitation, these Restrictions alone destroy every idea of an unlimited Freedom, and we beg leave to observe to you, that ill disposed servants under the cloak thereof, may always take advantage of us, and besides that, the former inconveniences may be revived under a new form.

The Great opinion which our Superiors (whom the knowledge of these particulars has reached) entertain of your just and

1. In the Maldah district.
2. In the Dinajpur district.

upright measures, and the Impression which they have already made upon us, leaves us no Room to doubt, but on the contrary to hope and expect, us the desired consequence thereof, your utmost endeavours to restore the country to its pristine State of *Lusture*, to re-establish its Finances and to support its Commerce, both so much fallen, and thus consequently to participate in like manner to the Dutch Company, by letting them enjoy the salutary effects and advantages that must necessarily arise from such wholesome and Prudent Measures; and to afford them such Ease and Conveniences in their Trade that their Residence in this Country may be made supportable to them, and that by a sufficient advance upon the Returns, the Course of *Busyness* may be again placed, in a better Light, your Honours can without doubt contribute immediately thereto, as well by an open acknowlegement of our here before mentioned Rights and Prerogatives, as by the *Existance* (? exercise) of the best means to prevent the infringements with which they may be attacked and by giving strict orders under Penalties to all such as shall directly or indirectly endeavour to prejudice us, and be of Hindrance to us, so as to disappoint and render abortive the general plan in view.

If your Honors would now be pleased to enter warmly into the Busyness, it speaks, as it were of itself, that this good intention will extend itself over our Trade throughout the whole country. We persuade ourselves that there would then be a greater facility in laying in the respective investment of silk and silk stuff, the difficulties *attendant* on which are of no less a weight and importance than in the other articles. In the year 1772 full representations were made thereof by our Chief at Cossimbuzar to the English Agents, as likewise to Mr. Hastings himself. In consequence of the orders given by his Honor an incredible alteration took place in the price of *Pattenys*[1] from 5 to 9 Tolas for the rupee and we make bold to assert, that a real freedom of Trade accompanied with an effective Prohibition and penalty upon all abuses, in particular such as happened in 1773, and have been thought of by Mr. Pattle, would have a further desirable Effect and contribute considerably to a reaso-

1. Vide Glossary.

nable Price for the *Pattenys* the Provision of which is of equal importance to both nations.

From the above conference held by our Chief at Cossimbuzar Mr. Ross with The Hon'ble Mr. Hastings, it appeared to us that the name of the Dutch Company had been used as a means of Imposition in the Trade or Provision of *Pattenys*, the English Gomastahs, in the year 1772 have given up as purchased for Account of our Company, the quantity of 2000 Maunds; whenever we can assure you that it was with the Greatest Difficulty we were able to procure 500 Mds. In order to remove this evil which is equally practised in Respect to the Silk stuffs, whereby more than one Hundred thousand Pieces were given up at making or our Company and in Fact only 3000 pieces furnished to us, the aforesaid Mr. Ross proposed an expedient to Mr. Hastings, that in case circumstances should absolutely require it, and the general freedom of Trade and Investment was no less and the Principal End, we should consider it as proper and suitable to the Times, but at that Juncture must regard it not only as an absolute constraint and limitation, but altogether unneedfull as it conveyed, an obligation compulsatory on us to give up to the English Agents & Gomastahs, the quantities of Silk & Silk Stuffs, that we might have occasion for, and of the Successive pareds (?) To be purchased, in order to comply therewith which would be inconsistent with freedom exclusive of giving Room for a Hundred Pretexts of rendering the investments difficult for us to procure, as has frequently been & is still the case, when notwithstanding a like arrangement had been spoken of & settled with Mr. Grueber, the English Gomastah, who informed us that our specifications or Indents had nothing to signify, and that in order to have no interruption in the Trade we must procure them a Perwannah from the above Mr. Grueber.

To be short Gentlemen, it is Chiefly the arbitrary modes of Trade practised by your own European Agents & servants, and the Fortunes & Artifices of the Natives in your employ, which being checked & set bounds to, and thereby Striking at the Root of the Evil, we might flatter ourselves, that advantage would be drawn from the plan in view. A strict compliance with the orders which you may give, will carry conviction with itself, and we flatter ourselves that Trade would then become as easy and practicable for Every one as it used to be, but that continual changes do not always effect the desired Reformation, is so incontestibly true, that we have no occasion to carry our attention further than to the late involuntary enormous Rise, of the *Haspelloon* under plea of the introduction of the new method of winding silk, wherein we have also been obliged to participate, that the Company's Busyness might not stand still from the Desertion of the Work People, altho' we have preserved the method of *Verhaspeling* upon the old Footing.

Ophium is an article in which the Company in former days carried on a considerable Trade. Since which oppressions have been committed & destructive monopolies been carried on in it, which have been hurtfull to the enterprisers themselves & others equally. Private merchants made use of violence & inveterate measures to secure to themselves the preference in this Trade and have thereby done it incredible prejudice. It was already carried to that Pitch that our. Gomastahs no longer durst receive any money from us in advance, and the little that could be got at, it were by contraband could be obtained only at the most enormous prices. The numbers of speculators & their modes of carrying on the trade absolutely prevented us from getting the quantity that was required of us to procure and purchase. The influence & Respect which all these encroaching Traders possess, not only ruins the Price but violence & oppression have in a considerable manner prevented & put a stop to the Culture of that valuable product, so that the Cultivator as well as the merchant, and the proprietor of the land is deprived of that advantage which they would otherwise most undoubtedly reap from so precious an article of Trade. We may therefore hope that also this point will excite your serious attention, not only so far as regards our investments, but for the particular Benefit of the Country, & its Revenues, that every Plan of monopoly & Exaction in this article may be defeated, and that we, who are permitted & authorised to purchase this article according to our own will from the first hand, may be enabled to provide without interception the yearly quantity that we may stand in need of.

In the Salt-Petre, we have been allowed for our share of the produce of Bihar the trifling quantity of 23000 Maunds. This

Maxim has been introduced since 1763 & 64 when it was imagined the English Company would renounce the exclusive privilege which had been granted to Lord Clive in the year 1758. It has however been all this Time deemed impossible to make any alterations, or fall upon any Plan or arrangement, more conformable to the Rules of Justice, not that there has been wanting complaints & Remonstrances on our parts, as appears form last year; When, you were pleased to say in answer that unless you fell short in your own Demands, there would be no alteration in it: therefore no fixed arrangement could be ever made. We beg leave to remark to you that this objection will lose much of its weight, if you would really please to do us justice. For you will please to consider in the first place how much the Province of Bahar produces yearly, and how much thereof is bought up & exported by the privileged individuals; in the next place, how that, in former Days, when both our Companys, together with that of the French were inside contract with each other, their Demands were fully satisfied from the General produce thereby that the Prohibition laid by you upon the sending of Salt-Petre not made in Suja ul Dowlah's country will answer little or not at all the intention, as it is the General Belief that Soujah ul Dowlah's provinces do not produce near so much as we think, is shipped off, under that name from Patna & in particular transported from the Country, all this impartially considered Gentlemen will convince you fully of the Justness & Propriety of our Complaints in regard to the small portion of Salt-Petre that is allotted us. We agree nevertheless that this question will naturally arise, whether the English East India Company considering its present situation has not a Right to a greater share in the Salt-Petre, than the other Nation equally privileged with them to make Purchase thereof? The exclusive Right, which after the capture of Calcutta they made themselves masters of, thro' Lord Clive furnished them as the Gentlemen Directors in England themselves have maintained the means, as in former Days were practised by Hadsje Ahmet[1] and Chodja Wazid[2] of monopolizing the Salt-Petre, and obliging others with it accord-

1. Haji Ahmad, brother of Nawab Alivardi.
2. Khawja Wajid, a principal merchant of Bengal.

ing to their Humours. But seeing that the said English East Indian Company has renounced that Right, that it has been their positive Direction that the Dutch Company should have an equal Right with them in Salt-Petre Trade as formerly; and that these orders have been repeated, nothing could be more just, more proper, and more consonant with or more necessary for the Benefit of Both, than the fixing upon a sufficient mode of making a partition of the produce with more Impartiality, and it was in that Expectation that in September 1766 we declared our opinion with confidence to Council of Calcutta, that in order to prevent an augmentation of Price in the Salt-Petre, it would be proper, that the Right of the aforesaid Perwannah should not be infrigned but that the Investment should be laid in by one of the European Nations for joint Account, the same as was done by agreement in the year, 1745. We remain still in those sentiments and we conceive that the contract made at that time might serve as a foundation, in case your Honours should think fit to treat further thereon, and would confer upon the Dutch Company an effective Freedom in that Article.

Exclusive of the above mentioned Encroachments upon their Trade, by which they must naturally have endured many disadvantages, the Company has been obliged to support the Expenses of their Establishment & further to submit to an annual unjust extortion at Patna, of more than Twenty Two thousand Rupees under the name of Paishcush: a contribution which upon strict Enquiry will be found never to have been lawfully levelled upon the Company, nor ever otherwise to have paid, than by compulsion, and a rigid exercise of power with which, since the introduction to this time, willing or unwilling, they have been obliged to acquisce, in order to avoid worse consequences. The unlawfull origin of the Paiscush was circumstantially represented in the year 1772, to the Hon'ble the Governor General Mr. Hastings by our Director Mr. Bacheracht and by our Chief at Patna Mr. Falck and we would expect nothing less could be expected from the shamefull continuance thereof, that we should prefer the most powerfull complaint and Remonstrance against it.

In the exercise of the Prerogative of Coinage we are frequently so circumstanced as to be embarrassed thro' Fear of

Loss : The privileges, whereof We speak, belongs to us, the Preference in the coinage above all others. By which we may carry the silver to the mint as it suits us. But how frequently has it happened that just as our work is finished and that we are provided with an immense quantity of Rupees or Siccas of the Current year, a fresh order is issued for the coinage of new Siccas, whereby ensues a loss by the Batta in the payment of the other. In such an Event the Company is exposed to a heavy loss upon their own money. The lowest Rate of Batta is in general from 2½ to 3 P. Ct. The Eleven and Twelve suns have now for these three years preserved an equal value in their Currency, notwithstanding the frequent attempts made to lessen that of the Former. Should now those of the Fifteen sun be issued out, as has been intended ever since last October the value of the Eleven and Twelve suns siccas will decline as usual, and because there are no Rupees coined of the 13 and 14 sun none been current for some time, they will soon be declared sonauts, which will occasion a very considerable Loss.

We are sensible that this is a general misfortune, and that the decrease in value of the *Specie* must be ascribed to the arbitrary mode of Trade among the covetous Shroffs and Bankers and others of that Stamp, but we ought to regard such meanness an extraordinary and Usurious profit, and equally a sore to commerce in General, as to every individual in particular, who frequently finds himself suddenly robbed of some percents in the value of his money which he cannot pay away without great loss, whilst some few are by those means hoarding up Riches. That this evil, altho, there may not be a possibility of wholly exterminating may nevertheless be reduced & set Bounds to, as by the order which was published in the year 1773, namely that the Rupees of the forgoing year should bear an equal value with those of the next year entered upon, and remain so till the Current year should be expired and people would be able to provide against the inconvenience thereof, if either a certain period was fixed for the alteration of the Coin or that publication should be made of new Siccas to be coined and issued when, if it should be required to postpone the same, in such case the Publick to be informed & made acquainted how long the Current Rupees could retain their Currency without being subject to a Batta. This would however in no wise prevent a loss arising to those who kept them to the last, for as the Period approached for the alteration to take place, no Shroff nor other Person would receive such Rupees, as we knew before hand, would in a few days be subject to a Batta, which necessarily would avoid much interruption in Trade. So Admirable an Institution must then be desirable as well for the sake of some powerful Banker & Dealers in Exchange, for the Publick good, that all were put upon a Footing, which is a considerable point in Trade, and for which the publick in general would esteem themselves obliged to your Honors.

We come now to the Point respecting the exercise of Justice over the Inhabitants concerning which altho' authorized thereto, we have frequently had disagreeable Breach and Disputes with the Fouzdar of Haughlee. People who call themselves our subjects and inhabitants, claim very readily our protection when they think it unadvisable to stand Loyal before the Moorish Judge, and how many Instances could not we produce that the Director has been prayed and solicited, to enquire into some of the disputes to judge of them according to Equity and to determine upon them from whence may be sufficiently deduced, that people have in Effect considered us as having a Right to the Exercise of Justice over our inhabitants, but above all the Sunnud granted to the Company in the year 1766 by the Nabob Self-ul-Dowlah[1], Seyd Nejubil Alli Chan, verbally says, "That neither the Fouzdar of Houghly nor his Dewan, nor any other of the inhabitants of Chinsurah, Mirzapore, and Barnagore as belonging to the Dutch Company, shall levy any fine or committ any assault, much less send their servants to apprehend, and bring before the *Durbar* of Houghly these or any of their Ryots, but all cases that come before them, must be left to the Decision of the Dutch Director, who, as often as the Fouzdar shall lay any complaints before him of these shall minutely and impartially enquire into the case."

Which very clearly fixes the power which we have over the inhabitants of our Colonies. How very opposite to all this, notwithstanding, has been frequently the will and inclination of

---

1. Saif-ud-daulah.

several Fouzdars that have since resided at Houghly ? How many Times has the Company's Trade not been threatened with the most fatal consequences by reason of Peoples speaking openly, against this Privilege which is so clear, in the view of weakening it ? We should pass beyond all the Bounds of Brevity which the present length here of Prescribed to us, if we entered into a Detail herein of every past circumstance. We chuse rather to let it rest there : But we presume from what has been already said, it may be proved that the Respective Fouzdars have no unlimited authority or free command over us and our Dependants. Criminal cases subject to corporal punishments, or Capital Delinquent excepted, We conceive we ought & may insist upon the undisturbed exercise of Civil Justice, carrying along with it the Punishment of crime which shall fall short of being Capital.

Upon this Head we urge you also Gentlemen, to consider seriously of this part of our privileges, and we request that you will, once for all, give to the Fouzdars, such strict and Positive orders, that we may thereby be preserved free from all captiousness, Chicanery. Troubles, inconveniences, Outrages and contempt, in a word from all Tyranny, vexatious suits and Molestations, which are destructive of all order and inconsistent with the very precious Rights we have obtained.

We request the like attention to our complaints in regard to the Number of *Chokeys*[1] that have been introduced here and there along the shore, and stop our vessels under vain and frivolous Pretences, as if they had a right to visit for whereas we might make good the payment of the Established duties at the old accustomed places of customs and for the Proof thereof provide our vessels with *Dusticks*[2] after shewing of which they should pass and repass, so that the aforesaid unlawful, Chokeys, that are introduced here and there along the shore would not assume to themselves, to stop our vessels for many days together and extort money from them, without complying with which they seldom or ever get off free; In fine what has been said is not only an Hindrance to the Company and individuals, but altogether unbecoming & therefore highly punishable.

---

1. Vide Glossary.
2. Vide Glossary.

Herein now Gentlemen our complaints seemed chiefly to be grounded. The Justice which we expect to have from applying to you for Redress is, as we have observed at the Beginning of this Memorial, founded upon the Hon'ble English Company having generally acknowledged that they have in the name of the lawfull sovereign of this country acquired to themselves the Government of the affairs that pertain to its Policy & Finances. We join thereto your own kind offers of Assistance for promoting the concerns of our Company, signifying to us in your letter of the 24th Octr. 1774 and also the Commands of your superiors, which you cannot be ignorant of that the Dutch Company *shall enjoy the like Freedom of Trade, safety & protection* with that of the English; and it remains with you to let us feel immediately & in good earnest the effect of so forcible a Recommendation.

We now conclude this memorial with one more proposition. The village of Bernagore (properly Baranegger) lying in the neighbourhood of Calcutta and thus very advantageous for your settlement. We tender to you in exchange and by way of Barter for as much Ground in the circle or environs of Chinsurah as Baranegger contain its full extent. On account of its great distance from us, and having no particular person to Govern them; the possession of it is of the less consequence to us, but of the Greater Importance to your Honors, on account of its aforesaid vicinity. You will therefore be pleased to take this proposal into consideration, and if it can with consistence, suffer it to take place. *Actum* in the Council Chamber at Houghly in Bengal the 10th April 1775.

Signed/—John Bacheracht,

J. P. Humbert, A. Bogaardt.
Will. Dankelman, J. Radermacher
&ca &ca &ca. ,,.

Appendix H

"To

The Honorable William Hornby Esqr.
President & Governor & ca Members of
the Select Committee in Bombay.

Hon'ble Sir and Sirs,

The occasion of this separate address, is, purposely to acquaint your Honor and etc. that some Dutch ambassadors from Cochin, accompanied by Isac Surgeon, have proceeded to Syringapatam, and there is great reason to suspect, have entered into a Treaty with the Nabob greatly to the prejudice of the Hon'ble Company's Interests on the Malabar coast, for Sir Adams informs me that a Scheme is on foot which only waits the approval and support of the General and Council at Batavia, some particulars of which Mr. Adams has secretly obtained and are as follows. "That the Nabob is to let the Dutch here all the Pepper and Sandlewood produced in his Country and they in return are to assist him in binding and fitting, at a fleet and to send to Syringapatam two hundred European soldiers, and a Dutch Commandant, and they have further engaged to assist the Nabob by land and sea to make a conquest of the Travancore Country.

The Ambassadors to return are to Syringapatam in six Months, for they conclude by that time the ships may arrive from Batavia with all the necessary means to carry the Scheme into Execution. But whether all this will really end in their Junction, as little time, will, I suppose investigate, tho' if one may prevent to form any judgment on the Nabob's conduct for sometime past there is reason to think he press some scheme in view to enlarge his Power on this coast, as he has lately sent down orders for building, & equipping 12 ships & Grabbs besides Gallivatte, at the Ports of Callicutt, Mungallore, Cundapore, and this place, & they are all actually in hand, which together with the Evasions he has used this season with the investment of Pepper & Sandlewood & the small Quantity of Sandal deli-

vered, & not any of the Sound of Pepper must at least denote the Nabob's indifference to continue on the friendly footing with the Hon'ble Company, tho' I must observe to your Honor and ca. their espousing the cause of Ragobah has advanced him so much already as to draw from him lately a Letter importing that he has issued strong orders for the 500 Ladies of Sound at Pepper being delivered us without Delay but I must presume to offer my opinion founded on a positive proof of his real character, that both the Dutch' Scheme noticed by Sir Adams and the future Treatment the Company expect to receive in this Country greatly depends on the termination of the Mahratta War. If our arms prove successful in establishing Ragobah in the sovereign authority at Poonah the Nabob will then be manageable, as he will, on the Contrary happening, be totally remindful of the Consequences that will result to the Company's settlements on this Coast from his leage with the Dutch, or indeed any other Power whom he can make to serve his present purpose.

I should before have mentioned in your Honor and ca that the Nabob has advanced to the Dutch ambassadors Ten Thousand Rupees by a Draft on his Governor at Callicutt in order to provide artificers for building his ships.

Thinking it my duty to lay this circumstances before you, I remain with the greatest respect.

Hon'ble Sir and Sirs,
Your most obedient Humble
Servant
Sd/-William Townsend"

Onore
8th May 1775

Appendix I

Parole Form :—The Dutch Fort at Chinsurah and its Dependencies, with its stores, effects, and merchandises, both public and private belonging thereto, or contained in them having surrendered to the arms of the Hon'ble the English East Company of Great Britain in consequence of a summons to that effect by Captain Charles Chatfield, commanding a Regiment of the said Hon'ble Company at Chandarnagore, and it having been granted that such of the inhabitants of the United States who shall give their Parole of honour to demean themselves according to such orders as shall be enjoined them may remain in possession their houses until further orders. I....of the said Fort and town of Chinsurah give my parole of honour neither directly or indirectly to do anything which may give offence, or do harm, to the said Hon'ble Company, or to the British Nation; I promise to be no wise concerned in, or be consenting to, the forcible or clandestine removal, diminution, or spoiling of any of the above-mentioned stores, effects or merchandises but will give immediate notice thereof to Messrs. Purling, Heatly and Adair....

Moreover I promise to surrender myself prisoner of war at Chinsurah whenever I shall be summoned, and till then to obey these and all other orders as shall be enjoined me by the Hon'ble the Governor General and Council at Calcutta, to whom I hereby give this my Parole of honour. In presence of....

These terms were granted and these restrictions enjoined by the Hon'ble Governor-General and Council in Calcutta and so to continue until further orders."

The same form, having changes only in place names, was prescribed for men of the other Dutch factories in Bengal.

Appendix J

A letter from Sir Edward Hughes, dated the 12th September 1782, giving an account of the operations of the squadron under his command and reviewing the circumstances under which Trincomalle fell into the hands of the French (Sec. Con. 3 Oct., 1782, No. 1).

"I had the honour to address you by letter dated the 8th of last month from this place and sailed hence with His Majesty's Squadron under my Command on the 20th using all diligence to get to Trincamale, but the Winds blowing much from the South I did not arrive off that place till early on the 3rd of this month when I found it in possession of the French and their Squadron reinforced by the Illustre' a 74 Gun Ship, the St. Michel a 64, the Elizabeth formerly a Company's Ship of 50 Guns, and many transports at an anchor in the several Bays there.

On the same day His Majesty's Squadron had a severe Engagement with that of the Enemy an account of which is herewith enclosed, and I am much concerned to inform you that on the morning of the 4th, I found the several ships so very much damaged in their Hulls and Masts as to render it impossible for them to keep the Sea, four of them the Hero. Burford, Monmouth and Eagle were with dfficulty kept above Water with all their pumps at work from shot holes so low down that it is found very difficult to stop them even an anchor in smooth Water, and all the ships have suffered so much in their masts, yards, and Rigging that the short time the Squadron can with safety remain on this Coast will be scarce sufficient to refit them for Sea. I was therefore under the disagreeable necessity Trincamale being lost, to proceed with the Squadron to this Road, and so very much were the ships disabled that it was with difficulty I made the land between Sadras and this place, and anchor'd here on the 9th of this month.

Before I sailed last from hence I ordered Captain Gower of His Majesty's Ship Medea to remain in this Road till the return of Sir Eyre Coote with the Army from the relief of Velour, and then to be assisting to Him in any operations he might prosecute to the Southward by convoying and covering any ships or vessels employed to carry Rice for the subsistence of the Army. On my return I found the Medea employed on this Service, and apprehending the Enemy might send some of their large Frigates immediately to the Coast, and probably ships of greater force when they get refitted, I have sent His Majesty's Ships Sceptre, Isis and Conventry to reinforce the Medea, and the Squadron being in the greatest want of Gunpowder, and this Presidency unable to furnish the supply requisite from the small stock they have of that article, I have sent His Majesty's Fire Ship the Combustion to Bengal, with orders to wait at Hedgerie, and earnestly request you will be pleased to order two Hundred and fifty thousand pounds of the best Gunpowder in your Magazines to be sent on board of her in Barrels of 100 pounds each if possible with all expedition in order that she may return to me here early in next month, as without that supply the Squadron cannot proceed to Sea the cost of the Powder shall immediately be paid to this Presidency.

I had the honour to receive on the 10th of this month your very obliging letter of the 7th of last, with copies of your letters of the 26th December last to the President and Select Committee of this Presidency and of the 25th March last to Captain Gregory of the Fortitude, and I return you Gentlemen my very hearty thanks for your kind Congratulations on the success of His Majesty's Squadron under my Command against the Enemy.

I am sorry that you have any reason to think you perceive the last instance of a want of Confidential intercourse between the Presidency of Fort St. George and myself, and assure you there is not the least ground for such a conjecture, my intercourse and correspondence with this Presidency is one entire and connected detail of the Operations of His Majesty's Squadron under my Command, of its wants, and my wishes, all of which have been duly attended to, as much as, I believe, was in the Presidency's power. I am equally happy in assuring you Gentlemen that the same friendly intercourse ever has, and does now, subsist between Presidency of Bombay and myself although the means of corresponding with that Presidency is less frequent than heretofore, or I could wish, and I beg of you Gentlemen to assure yourselves that, as it ever has been my practice since I have had the honour to command His Majesty's Squadron in the East Indies to conduct the Service of the Public as far as related to my Department, in perfect Harmony and Friendship with all the Presidencies, I shall use my best endeavours to continue to do so on every occasion.

The loss of Trincamalle is a misfortune to the Company's and the national Interests in this Country, that will soon be severely felt, the Enemy by getting possession of that Harbour so very capable of being defended, have a Post where they cannot only refit their ships at all times, but are thereby in a condition to continue in these Seas without returning to the Mauritius, by which their plans of Operation will become much more extended and certain; but that Trincomalle is lost is no fault of mine, but of those whose Duty it was to have placed a sufficient Garrison in it, which notwithstanding my almost daily representations of the great importance of the place was not done, and although the Squadron not only captured the place by great exertion from the Dutch, but afterwards covered it for six months against both French and Dutch whose intentions to recover it were open and declared, yet for other service was expected from me than barely the security of Trincamalle, and it became absolutely to attend to the operations of the Enemy's Squadron on this Coast which brought on the Engagement of the 6th July last, as the protection of Trincamalle has brought on that of the 12th April last, after the Engagement of the 6th July, state of the Ships of the Squadron both as to their Masts, Hulls, Rigging, and Provisions made it absolutely necessary that they should proceed to Madras, to refit and procure provisions, no supplies of either being to be had elsewhere and before the return of the Squadron to Trincamalle, only a few hours, the place was lost, as I before observed from the want of a Garrison competent to defend it : Had the expedition against Jafnapatam planned by Sir Hector Monro (Munro) after the capture of Negapatam been carried into execution, the place would have fallen into our hands and given great security to Trincamalle but it was dropt, and the Troops destined for that so usefull a service were sent to make an idle parade through the Tanjor Country when no Enemy was in it.

As yet I have heard nothing by which I can judge with any

certainty where our Reinforcements under the Command of Commodore Sir Richard Bickerton may now be—His Majesty's Armed Store ship the Minerva and the Company's ships Major and Nottingham are arrived here, and say they sailed in Company with him from Rio de Janeiro on the 3rd June last, and they and 5 more Company's Ships of the Convoy parted Company on the 23rd of that month in blowing Weather, the Lieutenant who commands the Minerva informs me further that he afterward left Company's Ship and came the outer passage, the Commanders of the Company's ships having first signified to him their intentions of going to Bombay. On the whole I think it is very uncertain if Sir Richard Bickerton will come on this Coast, now that the season is so far advanced and that he will in all probability go to Bombay where that Presidency will use every means in their power to detain him, for its safety, or some co-operation with their Troops, this is however only supposition, and I shall wait his arrival on the Coast till the 15th of Next month, when I must proceed to Bombay with the Squadron for its security and repair, without which many of the Ships must be totally lost to the Service."

Appendix K

"We receive with satisfaction the kind testimony which your Excellency has afforded of the Treatment received by the French Prisoners from our Government. Our concern indeed for the comfort and happiness of the French within these provinces has not ceased with the conclusion of the War; It yet continues, and we have the pleasure to assure ourselves from the sentiments which your Excellency has expressed, and the Humanity with which your Excellency's character is so honorably marked, that your attention to the Prisoners of our Nation would not have been less deserving of our applause had the situation of the two Governments been reversed.

Having done ourselves the Honor to reply to your Excellency's letter of the 10th Septr. our next wish is to draw your attention to a subject which has been brought recently, and in a particular manner before us by appeals from the Dutch Government of Batavia and Columbo, and is of interesting importance to your Nation and to our own as well as to the States of Holland.

We have perused and given due consideration to the correspondence that has passed between your Excellency and the Right Hon'ble Lord Macartney and the Select Committee of Fort St. George as low down as the 9th of last July (to which period only it has been yet transmitted to us) concerning the execution of the stipulations agreed upon in the late definitive Treaty between His Britannic and Most Christian Majesty, as far as the same respects the Restitutions to be respectively made by the Representatives of the two Crowns in India, and we have observed that, in consequence of some differences relative to the cession of Trincomalle and orders received by your Excellency on this subject, an end was put to the Negociations of the Commissioners appointed on the part of your Excellency, and on the part of Fort St. George, and the question referred to Europe for a final decision on it.

We are persuaded that had your Excellency known that the powers possessed by his Government gave it a control over the Acts & Proceedings of other Presidencies of the East India

Company your Excellency would have represented to us any subjects of Difference that impeded the execution of the Definitive Treaty instead of referring the same to Europe, Possessing those Powers we wish even at this Time to meet the Desire which we are sure your Excellency possesses to carry into effect the stipulations of the Treaty if the same can be done under the orders which you have received from France, and without waiting for the Replies to your last Dispatches.

To remove, therefore, all difficulties and to obviate all Misconceptions with respect to the intentions of the two Crowns in as far as the same respect the Definitive Treaty of Peace and Friendship between His Britannic Majesty and the Most Christian King signed at Versailles on the 3rd Septr. 1783 and the Peace subsequently concluded between His Britannic Majesty and the States General of the United Provinces, we have the honor to make the following Propositions to your Excellency for immediate Effect.

1st. We propose that in conformity to the Instructions which you received by the French Frigate Precience from the Mareschal de Castrues & which you have been pleased to state to the Presidency of Fort St. George, you do immediately deliver up the Fort of Trincomalle and its Dependencies to the Representives of the Dutch Government of Columbo.

2ndly

We propose that whatever Commissaries or Agents you may be pleased to appoint to deliver over Trincomalle to the Dutch may be likewise considered as executing that Office on the Part of the British Nation, and we hereby declare them to be fully authorised for that purpose.

3rdly

That you deliver over the Fort, Town and Districts of Cuddalore to such Agents as the Right Hon'ble the President and Select Committee at Fort St. George shall depute to receive the same, and that you receive from them their formal cession of Pondicherry.

If these Propositions should be acceptable to your Excellency, and you should agree to carry them into Effect, we request that you will send the necessary information thereof to the Right

Hon'ble the President and select Committee at Fort St. George who are informed of them, and directed in conformity to them, to depute Agents from that Presidency to receive the Fort, Town, and Districts of Cuddalore, and to make a formal cession of Pondicherry and the other Places and Districts which are by Treaty to be put into the possession of your Nation, and which are to be assigned over by the Nabob Walau Jah and the Rajah of Tanjore.

We have directed the President and Select Committee of Bombay to carry the Definitive Treaty into effect on the Western Coast on receiving advices from Fort St. George that it has been accomplished on that of Coromandel, and we have the Honor to assure you that we on receiving similar advices shall not allow the least delay in making Restitutions that are to be made in these Provinces; Commissaries will of course be appointed on the part of the French Nation to receive them.

We have addressed the Governor General and Council of Batavia and the Governor and Council of Columbo with information of these proposition, and do ourselves the Honor to enclose copies of our letters for your Excellency's perusal.

The Propositions are so plain that we trust no question can arise in respect to their intent, since the only object is to remove by an abbreviated process the difficulties which have hitherto precluded the execution of the Treaties by dispensing with the unnecessary Form of your delivery of Trincomalle to the Representatives of our Nation, for the sole purpose of enabling the latter to make the like cession, which ought to be done at the same instant of time, to the Representatives of the Dutch, a species of accuracy not only useless in itself, but obstructive of every substantial purpose of the Treaties concluded for the three National Establishments in India but if any questions of doubt should occur, upon this subject we request that your Excellency's correspondence on such subjects may be immediately with this Government.

Your Excellency will pardon us for observing that after so explicit a Declaration of our sentiments, and after so incontestible a demonstration of our readiness to carry into immediate execution, on the part of our Sovereign and Nation, as well as the English East India Company, the stipulations of the late

Treaties of Peace, no Blame can be henceforward attributed to the English for any delay in completing the wishes and solemn arrangements of our respective sovereigns and Nations. We wish to believe, indeed we are persuaded that as you alone possess the means of carrying into instant effect this great and salutary work, no unnecessary delay will attend its complete accomplishment and we hope that you will be further pleased to transmit accounts of the final and happy accommodation of all embarrassments on this important subject by the earliest conveyance to Europe."

(Letter to Marquis de Bussy, 23rd November, 1784).

Appendix L

"....It will have been known to your Excellency and Honors before your Receipt of this letter that some correspondence has passed between the Governor of Columbo and Lord Macartney, the Governor of Fort St. George, on the subjects of the 4th and 9th Articles of the preliminary Treaty between His Britannic Majesty and the States General, and particularly that Part of it which respects the cession of Trincomalle and you will also probably have been informed that a period was put to a correspondence on the same subject between the Marquis De Bussy and Lord Macartney by a reference of matter in dispute to the proper authorities in Europe.

The letter which we have had the Honor to receive from you as well as one which has been addressed to us by the Governor and Council of Columbo have brought this important subject recently and regularly before us.

It is our wish to evince to your Excellency and your Honors, that we are no less desirous, on the happy Termination of hostilities between our respective Nations, to remove, in as far as depends on us, every possible impediment to the entire re-establishment of that harmony which had so long prevailed between our Sovereign and the States General before the commencement of the War, than we shall be studiously attentive to the Rights of your Republic, and especially to rights that have their foundation in a solemn Treaty. Had we had the Honor of receiving your representations to us on the subject of those established by the later Treaty sooner, we should have been happy to have afforded you an earlier proof of our decided regard to these principles.

The orders that we have received from our superiors direct us to fulfill the stipulations of that Treaty and on this account as well as for the reasons which we have had the Honor of stating to you, we are ready to carry those stipulations into effect.

In a letter therefore which we have this day written to the Marquis De Bussy, we have proposed to him that, in conformity to the instructions which he received from France under date the 25th October, 1783, and communicated to the Presidency of Fort St. George, His Excellency do immediately deliver up the Fort of Trincomalle and its Dependencies to the Representatives of your Government at Columbo,—We have proposed also that whatever Commissaries or Agents His Excellency may be pleased to appoint to deliver over Trincomalle to the Dutch, may be considered as executing that office on the part of the British Nation and we have declared them to be fully authorised for that purpose.

It is merely possible that the Marquis De Bussy having referred to France the questions that arose between His Excellency and Lord Macartney in respect of Trincomalle, may be desirous of waiting for an answer to his Dispatches before he takes any further measures on that subject, but we are hopeful that this will not happen, and supposing the Reverse, after the explicit Declaration which we have transmitted to His Excellency of our Sentiments, and after so incontestible a Demonstration we have afforded of our readiness to carry into immediate execution the stipulations of the late Treaty of Peace, no blame can be henceforward attributed to the English for any delay in completing the wishes, and arrangements of our respective Sovereigns and Governments in Europe. In effect we have executed it as far as the execution can possibly rest with us by the Reference which we have implicitly made to the Marquis De Bussy—The rest depends on him. He alone possesses the Means of carrying it into execution, being in possession of the places which are to be ceded.

We are sure that Gentlemen at Chinsura will not omit to inform your Excellency and Honors of the early attention that we paid to your claims and to those of the Governor and Council of Columbo and the readiness that we declared to replace the Dutch Company in possession of Chinsura, and the Factories dependant upon it on the footing on which they formerly possessed that Establishment—But as the 9 Article of the preliminaries directs that the Restitutions and evacuations to be exchanged on the respective behalfs of your Nation and ours should be exchanged at the same periods as those between Great Britain and France, and as the Marquis De Bussy had not yet agreed to deliver up Trincomalle and Cuddalore, we were concerned that we could not consent to the formal and regular cession of Chinsura till we should hear from the Marquis De Bussy, to whom we promised to write for a Definitive Answer relative to the cessions stipulated to be made by the Definitive Treaty with France.

In the mean time however we agreed that the Gentlemen who had been authorised to receive back the Dutch Settlements in this country, should take possession of the warehouses belonging to your Company at Chinsura and land their goods, and establish their own laws and such regulations as they might think proper in every respect, but that of hoisting their colours in the place, or introducting any troops or military stores. We assured them of every just protection they required to themselves and their Trade, and that we should only station a commissary on our part at Chinsura to correspond with them and with us until matters might be finally adjusted with His Excellency the Marquis De Bussy, and with the Governor and Council at Columbo for a formal restitution of all your establishments in conformity to the 9th Article of the preliminaries between Great Britain and the States General.

The Keys of the Factory and public Warehouses at Chinsurah have accordingly been given up, and in consequence of the Desire expressed by the Gentlemen at that place, we have directed our commissary to deliver over the warehouses at Patna and Cossimbazar which formerly belonged to the Dutch East India Company to such persons as might be appointed by the Council at Chinsura to receive charge of them.

We have the Honor to transmit to you enclosed a translation of a letter that we have received from the Chief and Council at Chinsura, in which they render us their Thanks for our favourable and speedy determinations on the application made to us allowing at the same time full weight to the reasons assigned by us against a further compliance with them for the present." (*Letter to Batavia*, 23rd November, 1784. *Foreign Department Proceedings*, 23rd November, 1784).

Appendix M

(A) "Since the year 1740 the King of Maldivia he used to send his vessels and those that are under his jurisdiction consigned to the Dutch Factory here at Balasore, in consequence of this business the King himself granted a Parwanah and orders to all of his subjects, that every one who trades to this Balasore should always consign under the protection of our Factory by the enclosed Purwannah your honour &ca. will see the orders which contents in it.

From the year 1740 till 1772 during this period the vessels from Maldivia did accordingly come under the consignment of our Factory and protection, but one Mr. Mariott, the late English Resident here, who through bribing and many presents to the Maldivia men took some vessels under his protection so remained continually from 1722 till 1781 in the course of these 10 years few vessels only that were under their protection, and the same was with us of which Mr. Alexander De Costa could testify your honour &ca. the truth of it.

Since our Factory surrendered up in the late War to English and they having had in their possession from the year 1781 till January 1786 Mr. William Wordsworth the present English Resident here he sustained under his protection most of the Maldivia Vessels, and the Maldivia men enjoyed very little success in trading.

In the year 1786 on Maldivia's men arrival here they found that our Factory was restored in her former situation; most part of them came to me for protection, and I having no means that I could without fail differ with Mr. Wordsworth, as here in the Maharatta Durbar they do justice only to those who bribe them, therefore the Nackodas or Supurcargoes of the Maldivia Vessels requested me to write a letter to their King for they absolutely want to come in our Protection I in the same time thought that there is not a reason why should our Factory lose the privilege held in former time. In January 1787 I despatched a Wakeel[1]

1. Vide Glossary.

or Messenger from thither with a letter and a present to the King of Maldivia giving him an account of our former friendship and correspondence with him.

In the 26th September, 1787, arrived here 2 vessels from Maldivia who gave me intelligence with the success my Wakeel met there with Maldivias King!; and there were coming 6 vessels consigned under the protection of our Factory, by this information and as the monsoon of their arrival being nigh at hand I dispatched my nephew Cladius Passman to Bulramgurry by the mouth of the river in order to wait for the arrival of the vessels and to lend them assistance in coming in the River.

From this place to the mouth of the river there is at distance of 12 English miles a place called Bulramgurry where lays an old English house, a free lodging to all the nations in this place, of which people use to live there expressly to lend assistance to the vessels that go out and come in the River being close to the sea side, also myself I made very often use of that place in these 16 years of my Residency in this country, my nephew Cladius Passman and many other Moores[1] and Jentoos[2] who sheltered in that house owing on account of the heavy rains, Mr. Wordsworth spitefully sent an order to his people to drive out of the house my nephew and servants and prevent communication between them and Maldivia men but not for the rest who remained there, however my nephew and my servants instantly quitted the house and retired into the Maharattas Ground to prevent Wrangles.

On the 5th and 6th Instant arrived in this Road 6 vessels consigned under my protection from the King of Maldivia and one of their boat or pinness was coming in the river enquiring after my people and notifying of their arrival, Mr. Wordsworth's people seeing this violently came up to my nephew and servants, while they were in the Maharatta Ground used hostility prevented my people communicating and giving any kind of assistance in the same day at 6 O' clock in the evening these vessels rode up the river in consequence of this information of the Nakhodas or supercargoes of the vessels that the King of Maldivia con-

1. Muhammadans.

2. Hindus.

signed the above 6 vessels to the Dutch Factory and by the letters of consignments orders represented to my Nephew by my Wakeel come from Maldivia, he and servants went on board of those vessels.

Now I must beg leave to lay before your honour &ca. this unmanly inhuman and unlawful conduct of Mr. Wordsworth's people who absolutely went on board those vessels (as if) it were their own, or consigned to them, severely beated my people out of the vessels this unjust cause and injuries I reported to Fousdar[1] he plainly said me that he does not wish intermeddle in this affair, therefore I may seek redress with my superior.

Among the 12 vessels arrived this year from Maldivia there is not one consigned to Mr. Wordsworth neither they have any inclination to be under his protection but forcibly through bribing the Fousdar ; took 6 vessels in his possession, the remainder vessels consigned to Mr. Wordsworth took Prisoners and supercargoes and tried to keep them in his favour but finding through their Industry and many presents did no effect kept the poor people in prison for a whole day and night, in the following day placed this supercargoes under the Guard of the sepoys and sent them on board of their vessels in order to bring up the River.

On the 11th instant the remainder 3 supercargoes that were with me, Mr. Wordsworth's people sent sepoys on board of their vessels took some of his people prisoner, upon which these supercargoes enquired after their people Mr. Wordsworth's people used the hostility in public upon which I thought it advisable to take my Wakull and the letters orders he brought from the King of Maldivia for me, and carried into Maharatoes Durbar where they made it peruse in public, wherein they understood that the King &ca. consigned to our Factory 6 vessels and recommended to my care and requesting my best endeavours in despatching soon as convenient, that he will in the approaching year if met success he will consign every vessel belonging to him.

The Fousdar seeing the just and reasonable privileges held formerly by our Factory, warn to Mr. Wordsworth's Wookeel (vakil) not make any trouble with the vessel come consigned to

1. Faujdar.

the Dutch Factory, Mr. Wordsworth's Wookeel upon which replied that Mr. Wordsworth desired him to express that he will by no means suffer a single vessel go under the Dutch Protection.

As never in this part of the world happened any of the like, which has kept me solemn without informing your honour &ca. of this piece of business, otherwise if I knew it a little of what I am now suffering, I would long before this have acquainted your honour &ca. with, however I thought the matter would at last settle here amicably with Mr. Wordsworth, but to the contrary on Mr. Wordsworth's absence who join to Calcutta in the 10th instant, his people acted with such outrage that I want words to express your honour &ca. they forced and took 5 vessels out of the 6 came consigned to our Factory, against the will of the supercargoes and carried people to the Maharatres Custom—house upon the vessels, and settled the Imort duty under the name of the English Factory, also transported the Cargo of Couries (*couries*) into their Factory, the remainder one vessel in which my Wakeel came from Maldivia, after they consigned plain seapoys on board and did all the possible they can to take in their possession through the power of Fousdar and capaciting the supercargo with present and at last with menace, upon which the supercargo of this vessel entirely resolved to leave Balasore unless they fall by force under the English protection, the Fausdar seeing their firm resolution strictly order the English Sepoys to quit the vessel and send the people of the custom—house and settled the import duty under the name of our Factory and delivered up the vessel to me.

Mr. Wordsworth's people seeing all their labour towards this single vessel proved fruitless invented a new method in preventing this vessel getting cargo and to proceed her voyage, the all sorts of provisions comes from the Maharatoes extent and they knowing most part of our Factory stand surrounded by the English Factory and only part stand open by the River way, therefore they thought to hinder the Cargo of the vessel coming through their Ground, I am no way dubious of their doing so as, it is not a great matter they committed against our Factory.

I further beg leave to inform your honour &ca. that this consignment of the vessels from Maldivia is no more than a honour to our Factory, but the benefits of it is very little, I must particularly beg that your honour &ca. will not think it is amiss for my troubling with this piece of business, which has come so unwilling and unexpected to me, though I did my best endeavour in keeping myself free from all their wrangles, but their envious heart is so far advanced that they intend to take our privilege and jurisdiction, in defending with reasons they designedly seek after one in doing mischief.

I must not omit informing your honour &ca. that all my constant labour and industry in disbursing out of my own pocket and in my own account a considerable sum of money, this merely proceeded writing to prove how ardent is my wish in restoring the right and property of our Factory took from us by others in the late War.

I hope your honour &ca. will not think of what I mention here are dubious for I have not yet set in this paper half of what has been past between me and Mr. Wordsworth and his people, therefore I most earnestly request your honour &ca. will be so graciously pleased to take the foregoing cause into your consideration and do as seem meet for the honour and benefit of our Factory, otherwise the things will by degrees turn worse and worser, by giving your honour &ca. this piece of trouble it is not that I wish myself to enjoy it, but it will also serve for great use to him who will succeed me hereafter therefore I freely venture to say that if your honour &ca. have any dubious to this my complaint the French Chief, and Danish Resident, they will answer as an evidence if required likewise, the enclosed letters &ca. from the King of Maldivia will prove also for the same." (Letter from Lawrence D'Costa to Isaac Titsingh, Governor and Members of the Council at Chinsura, dated Balasore, 23rd October, 1787).

(B) "In a letter dated 23rd of October last 1787, I have had the honour to petition your honour &ca. my just cause and reasons and the unjust hostilities I was suffered by Mr. William Wordsworth the English Resident here, as it being now again the commencement of the arrivals of Maldivias vessels it appear to me they freshly begin with double vigour of oppression than the former, but this, merely proceeded for the following reasons to wit.

My complaint to your honour &ca. it did take no place

through your honour and deliberation it was deemed a matter none concerned to the Company but my private affair, seeing what was happened to me last year I made myself quite silent, last night a Maldivias boat arrived in the Gaut[1] of our Factory and the people of her came to me with the complaints of their supercargoe saying that their vessels were consigned to me by their owner upon which Mr. Wordsworth's people boldly came into our ground even to the Gate of the Factory pulled out the Maldivia people and sent seapoys to the board of the vessel and to bring under his custody and now intended to use worse than he has done me last year.

As this public action and hostilities towards me are so enormous, and not a thing concealed to the world here of this open shame the Maharatoes Government as public they think of your Agent here so little that I want words to express your honour &ca.

But thinking what may happen hereafter, perhaps upon my own affair or our Factorys it cannot keep me silent without humbly entreating that your honour &ca. will take into the consideration pitying towards this my unfortunate case wlll be so graciously pleased to write a letter to Mr. Wordsworth or to the Governor General of Calcutta for my redress that, Mr. Wordsworth may not deprive me again with the vessles come under my name.

Your honour &ca. has been pleased and appoint me here for your Agent therefore, my sole dependence relied on your goodness being my benefactors and protectors which encourages me to assure that your honour &ca. will this time keep me under the shelter of your wings that I may not be robbed again by my oppressor of what is my right.

In case your honour &ca. should think my requests not worth your attention and not wishing to trouble yourselves with it, in this I earnestly entreat your goodness will permit me to claim a Right redress by applying to the Governor General of Calcutta with a Letter of Complaint.

I further beg leave to petition your honour &ca. will favour me with an answer as this affair is a matter that must be settled in the latter end of this month therefore I leave to your honour

1. Vide Glossary.

&ca. consideration, otherwise, my enemies will entirely take possession and deprive me for ever in all the steps I may undertake hereafter." (*from same to same*, dated 10th October, 1788.)

Appendix N

Cowries were used by the people of Bengal and several other parts in India for their ordinary, and also at times for their large, monetary transactions, at least from the 17th century,[1] if not earlier, till the early years of the 19th century, and their use as such gradually disappeared after that period. So a large quantity of *cowries* was imported by them from the island of Maldives.[2] Manucci (1653-1708) writes that *cowries* "came from the Maldives and are current money in the kingdom of Bengal". There are references to the sale of *cowries*, imported from the Maldives at different places in Bengal, in Fort William Consultations, dated 14th March, 1717[3], 16th June, 1718,[4] 14th October, 1720[5], and 29th May, 1721[6]. In their letter to the Court of Directors, dated the 10th December 1738, the Council in Calcutta observed : "Wrote to Ballasore for 80 Ton *cowries*, the ship by whom they were expected from Maldiva lost her passage and was forced into Ganjam, but 3 sloops are arrived with Cowries at Ballasore from her......".[7] In 1741-42 the "price of cowries broke at 33 pun[8] for a Madras rupee" owing to the arrival of two ships from the island of Maldives on the 12th September, 1741.[9]

In September, 1746, Mr. James Altham, Chief of the English Factory at Balasore, wrote to the Council in Calcutta for a supply of Rs. 15,000 to purchase cowries and to defray the expenses of his factory. The Council sent to him the required

1. Travels of Peter Mundy, Vol. II, p. 311.
   Tavernier (Ball's Edition), Vol. I, p. 413.
2. Bowrey, The Countries round the Bay of Bengal, 1669-79, p. 200; Hedges Diary (Hakluyt Publication), Vol. I, p. 96.
3. Wilson, Early Annals of the English in Bengal, Vol. II, part I, p. 263.
4. Ibid, Vol. III, p. 40.
5. Ibid, p. 283.
6. Ibid, p. 347.
7. Ibid, para 22.
8. Vide Glossary.
9. Bengal Letter to Court, 3rd February, 1743, para 65.

sum "for the running charges of the factory". But as *cowries*, imported from the Maldives, were then available in Calcutta at a cheaper rate, that is, 38 *pun* for a *Madras* rupee, they decided to purchase 25 tons of these in Calcutta and instructed Mr. Altham not to buy any quantity at Balasore.[1] As a matter of fact, the value of *cowries* fluctuated in Bengal according to the demand for them and their quantity available in the market.[2] Bolts estimated the value of 4,000 to 5,800 *cowries*, Stavorinus that of 4,800 to 5,200 and Rickards that of 2,560 to be equivalent to one current rupee. Milburn[3] in 1813 thus reckoned their value :—

"4 *Cowries*	.. equal to	1 *Gunda*
20 *Gundas*	.. "	1 *pun*
4 *puns*	.. "	1 *Anna*
4 *Annas*	. "	1 *Kahun* which is about ¼ of a rupee."

There are relevant references in the works of some contemporary writers about the almost universal use of *cowries* as the lowest medium of exchange in Bengal throughout the 18th and early 19th centuries[4]. The Dutch traveller Stavorinus, who visited Bengal in 1770-71, writes : "Copper coin is not seen in Bengal. For change they make use of *cowries*." It was only due to some inconvenience in the exchange of *cowries* that the use of copper coins was sought to be introduced by the English East India Company in Bengal in 1757. In that year Captain Brohier, Engineer in charge at the construction of a fort at Berhampore in the Murshidabad district, wrote to Mr. Roger Drake, President of the Council in Calcutta : "The payment of artificiers and coolies in *cowries* being extremely tedious, it would be necessary absolutely to coin annas either in silver or copper..".[5]

---

1. Bengal Letter to Court, 30th November, 1746, Para 19.
2. Wilson, Early Annals of the English in Bengal, Vol. III, p. 40 and p. 283.; Milburn, Oriental Commerce, Vol. II, p. 108.
3. Ibid.
4. For opinions of some of them vide J. C. Sinha, Economic Annals of Bengal, pp. 64—65 footnote and K. K. Datta, Bengal Subah, Vol. I, pp. 250—52 and pp. 457—64.
5. Proceedings, 13th October, 1757 : Long, Selections from Unpublished Records of Government, Vol. I, pp. 104—105.

But the plan did not evidently produce satisfactory results. Thus Captain Brohier observed in one of his letters to the Council in Calcutta in 1760 : "......the coolies and artificiers complain that they do not get the real value of the copper money they are paid in at the bazar".[1]

---

8. Ibid, p. 211.

Appendix O

English Version of the Proclamation

"Whereas armed Force acting under the pretended authority of the persons now exercising the Powers of his Britannic Majesty's ancient allies, their High Mightnesses, the States General of the United provinces, and has forcibly taken possession of the seat of Government, whereby the Stadholder has been obliged to leave his own country and to take refuge in Great Britain, We do by this Proclamation issued in virtue of His Majesty's Commands, invite and require all Commanders and Governors of Settlements, Plantations, Colonies and Factories in the East Indies, belonging to the said States as they respect the sacred obligation of honour and all allegiance fidelity to their lawful sovereigns (of their adherence to which they have at all times given the most distinguished proofs) to deliver up the said Settlements, Plantations, Colonies and Factories into His Majesty's possession, in order that the same be preserved by His Majesty until a general Pacification shall have composed the differences now subsisting in Europe, and until it shall please God to re-establish the ancient constitution and Government of the United Provinces, and in the meantime we do hereby promise upon the assurance of His Majesty's Royal Word that so long as the said Settlements, Plantations, Colonies, and Factories shall continue to be possessed by his Majesty, they shall be held and treated upon the same Terms with respect to all advantages, privileges, and Immunities to be enjoyed by the respective Inhabitants upon which the Settlements, Plantations, Colonies and Factories in the East Indies are held and treated which are now subject to his Majesty's Crown, or are otherwise possessed by the Company of Merchants trading from England to the East Indies under His Majesty's Royal Charter."

Appendix P

"The state of affairs in Holland having induced the Prince Standholder, who has retired to England, to give orders for the admission of British Troops into the several Dutch Settlements in India, for their protection, against the French, the Governor General in Council is pleased to desire that you will communicate them to the Chief of the Dutch Factory at Patna with a requisition to him to deliver up that settlement, on the Terms and conditions specified in the enclosed Proclamation to be held in the name of His Britannic Majesty, under the condition of its being restored at the conclusion of a General Peace, by which the Independence and constitution of the Republic, as guaranteed in 1788, shall be maintained and secured.

In the event of this requisition being complied with, you will take possession of the Factory, in the name of His Majesty, hoist the British flag there, and cause the Proclamation to be publickly read.

In the event of a refusal on the part of the Dutch Chief to comply with your requisition for delivering up the Factory to our temporary possession, you are to forward the enclosed letter to the Commanding Officer at Dinapore, who is directed therein to detach a Military Force to take possession of it, and to deliver up the keys to you.

This having been done, you will take an Inventory of the Public Property and effects at Patna, and instead of the proclamation abovementioned, you will issue one, on your own part omitting such of the clauses as have relation of the continuance of the Dutch administration, and stating the following :

That the Law and Customs shall not be infringed.

That no fresh taxes or Duties will be imposed.

That Permission will be granted to the subjects of the United States to trade to and from the English Company's Settlements with the same advantages as the subjects of the most favoured nation, and every endeavour will be used to promote, in their behalf the extension of these advantages in the most liberal manner.

You will be particularly observant that the Inhabitants are treated with attention and kindness and you will assure them that they may depend upon both.

One copy of the Inventory is to be attested by the Dutch Chief and transmitted to me. The other copy is to be attested by you and delivered to him. The public Property and Effects are to remain in your custody, subject to our future orders, and you will advise us of any and what, articles appear to you to be in a perishable state, or might suffer by being kept.

Your future correspondence on the subject of the Dutch Factory at Patna is to be carried on with Mr. Birch the Commissioner for Chinsurah and its Dependencies, and you will attend to any communications you may receive from him upon it."

(Letter from G. Hay, Secretary to Government, dated, 14th August, 1795, to H. Douglas).

Appendix Q

"To

His Excellency &ca.

My Lord,

Para. 1. We have the honor to acknowledge the receipt of your letter from your Lordship in Council under date the 26th of October, conveying your instructions for the restoration of such Settlements and Factories as were in possession of the Dutch in the year 1803, and are now situated within the limits of our Authority.

„ 2. The Dutch not having had possession of any Settlement or Factory on the Coast of Coromandel or Malabar in the year 1803 we are led to conjecture that no restitution to the Netherlands Government are to take place in this part of the Peninsula of India, excepting that some compact to that effect has been concluded of which we are here entirely ignorant.

„ 3. We beg therefore to be furnished with such specific information upon the subject as shall enable us to ascertain the extent of the restitution to be made to the Dutch.

We have &ca.,

Fort St. George (Signed) H. Elliot
29th November, 1816. I. Hislop
B. Fullarton
Rot. Alexander."

2. "To the Right Hon'ble Hugh Elliot &ca,,

Hon'ble Sir,

We have had the honor to Receive your Dispatch of the 29th Ultimo relative to the Dutch Settlements on the Coasts of Coromandel and Malabar.

2. By the first article of the Convention concluded between His Majesty and the Government of the Netherlands on the 13th of August 1814 it is stipulated that all the Colonies, Factories & Establishments, which were possessed by Holland at the Commencement of the late war, in the Seas & on the Continents of

America, Africa & Asia with certain exceptions specified, that be restored to that Power.

The only exception on the continent of Asia is the settlement of Cochin which is ceded to the British Government in exchange for Banea & the petty settlement of Bernagore. It is true that none of the Dutch Settlements on the continent of Asia were in the possession of the Dutch at the commencement of the late war in the restricted sense of the term but it must be presumed, & this construction is confirmed by other parts of the Convention, that the restitution is meant to extend to all the Dutch possessions of which the restoration was provided by the conditions of the Treaty of Amiens, although not actually carried into effect. The very circumstance of a special provision being made for the cession of Cochin (which had been in our possession since its original occupation) to the British Government proves the correctness of this Construction, since that Settlement in common with the others was in our occupation on the 1st of January 1803, the dated assumed in the Convention as that of the commencement of the War.

3. We have acted on this construction of the Convention with regard to Malacca & propose to do the same with regard to Chinsura, & we can have no hesitation in authorising you to restore to the officers of the King of the Netherlands properly empowered to receive them all the Factories, Colonies & Establishments of the Dutch situated within the limits of your authority with the exception of Cochin.

We have & ca.,
(Signed) Moira

Fort William
Decr. 17th, 1816

N. B. Edmostone
A. Seton
G. Dowdeswell."

BIBLIOGRAPHY

A. Manuscript records.

(I) Record of Public Department. These include *Consultations, General letters to and from the Court of Directors* and various other papers and correspondence (National Archives of India).

(II) Bengal Secret Consultations, 1760-65 (National Archives of India).

(III) Records in the Foreign Branch of the Government of India, 1783-1825 (National Archives of India).

(IV) Correspondence of the Judge-Magistrate of Patna, 1790 onwards.

(V) Letters in the record-room of Cuttack Collectorate.

B. Published records.

(I) Rev. J. Long, *Selections from Unpublished Records of the Government of India.*

(II) S. C. Hill, *Bengal in 1756-57*, Vols. I. II. III. (Indian Records Series).

(III) *Bengal and Madras Papers*, Vols. II. III. (Government of India Publication).

(IV) *Midnapur and Chittagong District Records* (Bengal Secretariat Press Publication).

(V) *Original Papers relating to the disturbances in Bengal from 1759-1763*, Vols I and II. Published in London in 1765 A. D. (National Library, Calcutta.)

(VI) W. K. Firiminger, *Fifth Report*, Vols I—III.

(VII) *Select Committee's Proceedings in the year 1758*, edited by W. K. Firminger (Bengal Secretariat Press Publication).

(VIII) *Calendar of the Persian Correspondence*, Vols. I—VIII.

(IX) S. C. Hill, *An abstract of the Early Records of the Foreign Department, Part I*, 1756-1762.

(X) '*Clive's Narrative*' in Malcolm, *Life of Clive*, Vol. II.

(XI) Madras Government Records. Hodgson's Report. Short Description of the Dutch Settlements.

(XII) List of Artiquarian Remains in the Presidency of Madras, Vol. 1, 1882.

C. **Works of contemporary writers and travellers** (histories, travels, memoirs, etc).

(a) Orme, *History of the Military Transactions of the British Nation in Indostan*, Vol. II.

(b) Capt. Cope, *A New History of the East Indies*. London, 1758.

(c) Stavorinus, *Voyage to the East Indies*, (1768-1771), Vols. I. II. III.

(d) Edward Ives' *Voyage from England to India* in the year 1754. London, 1773.

(e) John Zephaniah Holwell, *Indian Tracts*. London, 1774.

(f) J. Z. Holwell, *Interesting Historical Events relating to the Provinces of Bengal and the Empire of Indostan*, 3 parts. London, 1765-1771.

(g) *Vansittarrt's Narrative*, Vols. I. II. III. London, 1766

(h) Verelst, *A View of the Rise, Progress and Present state of the English Government in Bengal*, London, 1772.

(i) *Reflections on the present commotions in Bengal*, London, 1764.

(j) Scrafton, *Reflections on the Government of Indostan*. London, 1763.

(k) Scrafton, *Observations on Vansittart's Narrative*.

(l) Lieut. Col. Alexander Dow, *Hindostan* (translated from original Persian with dissertations of Dow), 1768.

(m) *Consideration on the present state of the East India Company's affairs*; by a person, now, and for a long time past, interested in them. London, 1764.

(n) Grose. *Voyage to the East Indies*, Vols, I and II. London, 1772.

(o) *A fresh complaint lately exhibited to the states of Holland and West-Friezland by the Dutch East India Company in Bengal*, London, 1762. .

(p) *Facts relating to the Treaty of Commerce concluded by Governor Vansittart with the Nabob of Bengal*, etc. London, 1764.

(q) *The Journals of Archibald Swinton* (published in Bengal: Past and Present, January-June, 1926).

(r) *The Diary of Ananda Ranga Pillai.*

D. *Siyar-ul-Mutakherin* (in Persian) by the Bihar historian, Ghulam Husain.

E. *Maharastrapurana* by Gangaram (in Bengali), written in 1751 A. D.

F. *Correspondance du conseil de Chandernagore avec divers, 2e partie.*

D. Secondary Works :—

(1) *Memoir of the Colonel Francis Forde* by Colonel Lionel Forde.

(2) Mill, *History of British India* edited by Wilson.

(3) Edward Thornton, *History of the British Empire in India*, 6 Vols. London, 1841.

(4) E. H. Nolan, *Illustrated History of the British Empire in India.* London, 1862.

(5) Peter Auber, *Rise and Progress of the British Power in India.* London, 1837.

(6) G. B. Malleson, *The Decisive Battles of India.*

(7) Captain Arthur Broome, *History of Rise and Progress of the Bengal Army.* Calcutta, 1850.

(8) H. W. Van Loon, *The Fall of the Dutch Republic.*

(9) J. E. J. Rogers, *Holland* The Story of the Nations Series.

(10) A. Rea, *Monumental Remains of the Dutch East India Company in the Presidency of Madras.*

(11) Mannual of Madras Administration, Vol. I. 1885.

(12) Malabar, Madras, two volumes 1887.

(13) The Madura Country, Madras, 1868.

(14) Henry Beveridge, *Comprehensive History of India*, 3 Vols. 1867.

(15) Gentil, *Memoires Sur L. Indoustan*, 1822.

(16) Sir G. W. Forrest, *Life of Lord Clive*, 2 Vols. 1918.

(17) G. R. Gleig *Memoires of the Life of the Right Hon. Warren Hastings.* London, 1841.

(18) Das Gupta, *The Central Authority in British India, 1774-85.*
(19) *Cambridge History of India*, Vol. V.
(20) Elphinstone, *Rise of the British Power in the East*, London, 1887.

GLOSSARY

Abwabs :—"Miscellaneous cesses, imposts and charges levied in addition to the regular assessment on the land."

Aurang (*Arangs*) :—"A place where goods are manufactured (for sale); a depot for such goods". During the Company's trading days" this term was also applied "to its factories for the purchase, on advances, of native piecegoods, etc."

Banyans (*Banians*) :—A Hindu merchant or shopkeeper. A Hindu servent "employed in the management of commercial affairs." Bolts writes : "A Banyan is a person * * by whom the English gentlemen in general transact all their business. He is interpreter, head-book-keeper, head secretary, head-broker, the supplier of cash and cash-keeper and in general also secret-keeper."

Bapari :— A trader.

Barkandaz :—"A matchlockman but commonly applied to a man armed with a sword and stick, who acts as door-keeper, watchman, guard or escort."

Bukshbunder :—Customs-office at Hugli.
(*Bakshbandar*)

Batta :—"Difference in exchange, discount on coins not current or of short weight." Also "the rate of exchange between rupees of different species." It meant also an extra allowance given to "officers, soldiers, or other public servants when in the field, or on other special grounds; also subsistence money to witnesses, prisoners and the like."

Chokey :—"A watch-house; a customs or toll station; a station of police; a lock-up, a station of palankeen-bearers, horses etc. A place where an officer was stationed to receive tolls and customs."

Cossid :— A messenger.

Croory (*Crori*) :—'A collector of ten millions of dams. A permanent revenue collector of a portion of country, under the older Muhammadan Government. He sometimes, for a trifle commission, made himself answerable for that amount." (Wilkins). Also "the possessor or collector of a Kror, or ten millions, of any given kind of money; it was especially applied as an official designation, under the Mohammedan Government, to a collector of revenue to the extent of a Kror of dams, or 250,0,00 rupees, who was also, at various times, invested with the general superintendence of the lands in his district, and the charge of the police; the latter was ultimately withdrawn from him, but the former continued till the downfall of the (Mughal) Empire" (Wilson).

Daroga :— "An overseer, or superintendent of any department."

Dustick (*Dastak*) :—"A passport, permit or order. The term usually meant the passport issued by the Governor of Fort William, or the chiefs of the English Factories, for the goods of the Company or of their servants which exempted them from the payment of duties."

Dewans (*Diwan*) :—"Native minister of the revenue department and chief justice in civil causes within his jurisdiction." "A minister, or chief officer of state. Under the Mohammadan Government it was specially applied to the head financial minister, whether of the state or of a province, being charged, in the latter, with the collection of the revenue, the remittance of it to the imperial treasury, and invested with extensive judicial powers in all civil and financial causes."

Delols (*Dalals*)—"An agent between buyers and sellers; a broker, a salesman."

Faujdar—"Properly a military commander or a military governor of a district.....Also used in Bengal, in the 18th century, for a criminal judge". "The chief magistrate of a large district called Chucla. Also an officer who would receive rents from the Zemindars and account for them to the Government. An officer in all great cities in charge of the police and having power to take cognizance of all criminal matters."

Gomasta—"An Indian commissioner, a factor or agent." Also "a clerk for vernacular correspondence."

Jagirdar—The holder of a Jagheer.

Jumma (*Jama*)—A total territorial assessment.

Kattabara—"A duty levied on new boats." *Vansittart's Narrative*, Vol. 1, XXVI.

Mutasaddies—"Writer or clerk in a public office; also a general name for all officers employed in keeping the account" of Government or of any person of consequence.

Nazarana—"Anything given as a present, or any sum paid to the Government, as an acknowledgment for a grant of lands or any public office."

Nazim—"The first officer of a province, also styled Nawab or Subahdar, in whose hands the executive power was vested"; "the lord lieutenant, viceroy, or governor of a province".

Parwanah—"An order, warrant, grant or letter under a great seal; a letter of authority from a superior to an inferior or dependant; a licence or pass."

Pattenys (*Pattan*)—Goods ordered for manufacture.

Peshcush—"A tribute, quit-rent, fine, or a present paid to Government, as an acknowledg ent for any tenure, etc."

Picars—Paikars. "A dealer, a shopkeeper, an intermediate dealer or agent, a broker; also one who goes about with goods for sale, a hawker, a seller."

Rahdarry—*Rahadari*. Tolls or transit duties.

Syre—During the 18th century the term Syre or Sayer "was applied to a variety of local imposts, but especially to local and arbitrary charges levied by Zamindars and other individuals with a show of authority, on all goods passing through their estates by land or water or sold at markets (bazars, hauts, ganges) established by them."

Sircar—"The state, the Government, the supreme authority. Also under-banyans of European gentleman : also a domestic servant who is a kind of house-steward, and keeps the accounts of household expenditure, and makes miscellaneous purchases for the family : an Indian accountant in merchant's offices or a native employed in making purchases." "Also certain extensive administrative divisions of territory."

Soudagar—A merchant.

Vakil—"An attorney, or an agent or ambassador sent on a special commission, or residing at Court." "One invested with authority to act for another."

INDEX

C

D

N

Z